The Curse of Charley Butters

Collecting:
The Disappearance of Charley Butters, 2015
The Search for Charley Butters, 2016
The Death of Charley Butters

Library and Archives Canada Cataloguing in Publication

Worton, Zach, 1977-, author, illustrator
The curse of Charley Butters / Zach Worton.

Sequel to: The search for Charley Butters.
ISBN 978-1-77262-022-1 (softcover)

1. Graphic novels. I. Title.

PN6733.W67C87 2018 741.5'971 C2018-900207-7

First Edition
Printed by Gauvin Press, Gatineau, Quebec

Published by Andy Brown at Conundrum Press, Wolfville, NS, Canada
www.conundrumpress.com

Conundrum Press acknowledges the financial support of the Canada Council for the Arts, The government of the province of Nova Scotia, and the Government of Canada through the Canada Book Fund toward its publishing activities.

THE CURSE OF CHARLEY BUTTERS

part one
"the disappearance"

ALRIGHT, LET'S GET THIS OVER WITH, JERKS.

COME ON, TRAVIS! WE NEED TO USE THE DAYLIGHT!
GIMME A BREAK! I DON'T GOT THE LUXURY OF DOING MY MAKE UP ON THE WAY OVER HERE! I HAD TO GIVE DIRECTIONS!

HEY GUYS? YOU ABOUT READY TO GO?

YEAH, WE'RE JUST WAITING FOR LORD MAYBELLINE OVER HERE!
FUCK YOU GUYS!!

AND SO...

I CAN'T BELIEVE YOU GUYS RUSHED ME LIKE THAT! MY MAKE-UP'S NOT FINISHED AND NOW WE'RE GOING TO HAVE TO TAKE MORE TIME OUT OF SHOOTING!
DON'T WORRY, YOU CAN FINISH WHILE I SET UP.
JESUS CHRIST, TRAVIS! QUIT WHINING! THE REST OF US WOULD LIKE TO HAVE SOME FUN TODAY.
I AIN'T WHINING... I'M JUST... STATING FACTS. SHEESH.
YOU GUYS ARE SUPPOSED TO BE A BLACK METAL BAND! START ACTING LIKE IT, GOD DAMMIT! FUCKIN' LADIES SEWING CIRCLE.
ALRIGHT, ALRIGHT! I GET THE FUCKING POINT!! LET'S JUST GET THERE IN PEACE, OKAY?
HEH HEH

HEY, THE FIRST PLACE TO FILM IS RIGHT UP HERE. TIED UP A RIBBON AS A MARKER.

HERE IT IS!
WHOA! THIS IS FUCKIN' WICKED!

SO... STUPID... BETTER LAY IT ON THICK FOR THE BABIES.

YOU DID GOOD MAN! FEELS LIKE WE'RE IN AN ANCIENT TIME! TOTALLY PAGAN!
JESUS CHRIST. WOULD YOU GUYS GET READY SO WE CAN SHOOT THIS THING?!
JEEZ, RELAX MAN. WE'RE JUST TRYING TO HAVE A LITTLE BIT OF FUN HERE!
I CAN APPRECIATE THAT BUT WE'RE GOING TO START LOSING DAYLIGHT IN A COUPLE HOURS. JUST ... GET READY.
MAN, FUCK THAT GUY! WE'RE GONNA DO THIS AND IT'S GONNA RULE. IT'S GONNA BE FUCKIN' EVIL!!

BUT AT NIGHT IN THE DARK WE CAN MAKE THIS THING LOOK TOTALLY BAD ASS!
DO YOU SEE ANY LIGHTS HERE? AM I SUPPOSED TO FILM YOU GUYS AND HOPE YOUR MAKE UP REFLECTS THE LIGHT AND ALLOWS MY CAMERA TO CAPTURE IT? NOT BLOODY LIKELY!

SO WE'LL FILM BY THE LIGHT OF A BONFIRE. AND WHY DO YOU HAVE TO BE SUCH A DICK?!
BECAUSE WE HAVE TO START FILMING THIS NOW! YOU GUYS CANNOT AFFORD ME FOR MORE THAN A DAY! NO, SCRATCH THAT, AN AFTERNOON!

YOU ARE IN AN UNDERGROUND BLACK METAL BAND FROM A SHITTY SUBURB OF TORONTO--
WHAT DOES WHERE WE'RE FROM MATTER?

HOW MANY PEOPLE COME TO YOUR SHOWS?
OUR FAN BASE IS NOT CANADA, MAN! WE DO PRETTY WELL IN EUROPE THOUGH.
ANSWER THE QUESTION!

SORRY, I HATE TO INTERRUPT BUT WE COULD BE FILMING RIGHT NOW IF IT WEREN'T FOR YOUS TWOS FAGS' YACKIN'! WE BEEN STANDING HERE FOR LIKE 5 MINUTES LISTENING TO YOU GUYS BICKER!

NOW, YOU TWO HAD BETTER KISS AND MAKE UP SO WE CAN FINISH MAKING THIS VIDEO!
GRMBL
FINE.

NOW COME ON... KISS.

WELL, NOW THAT'S TOTALLY UNCALLED FOR!!

AND SO...
CLIK

OH YEAH... LOOKS GREAT.

ALRIGHT...
HOW DO YOU GUYS FEEL ABOUT MOVING ON TO THE NEXT LOCATION?

HEY, WHAT'S THAT OVER THERE?
SHRUG

JUST LOOKS LIKE A SHACK TO ME.

LET'S GO LOOK! MAYBE THERE'S SOMETHING TOTALLY WEIRD WE CAN USE!!
YEAH, GOOD THINKING!

Y'THINK ANY ONE LIVES HERE? I MEAN IT IS KINDA RUN DOWN.
IT DOESN'T LOOK LIKE ANY-ONE'S LIVED HERE FOR A LONG TIME.
KNOCK KNOCK
UM--NO ANSWER.
SEE IF IT'LL OPEN.
STUCK!

WHMP

GRMBL
JESUS CHRIST! LOOK AT THIS PLACE!

HOLY SHIT. I THINK THESE NOTEBOOKS ARE FROM THE 1950'S.
WOW, LOOK AT ALL THESE.
I DON'T UNDERSTAND WHY THERE ARE HUNDREDS OF THE SAME PAINTING!

SOUP FROM THE 60'S. I WONDER IF IT'S WORTH SOMETHING?
UNLESS WARHOL DESIGNED IT, I'M GOING TO SAY NO.
SHITTY.

OK, LISTEN TO THIS: "MAY 18, 1959. THE OPENING WAS A HUGE SUCCESS FOR ME! 10 OF THE 15 PIECES SOLD AND THAT WAS ONLY THE FIRST NIGHT!"

"THE SHOW IS UP FOR ANOTHER MONTH, TOO! IT WAS PACKED TO THE GILLS AND THERE WERE SO MANY INTERESTING FOLKS FROM THE LOCAL ARTS COMMUNITY! BEAUTIFUL WOMEN AND EVEN A FEW CRITICS!"

"AT ONE POINT THAT EVENING A FAIRLY REPUTABLE ART DEALER PULLED ME ASIDE--"

SO-UH-WHO IS THIS GUY ANYWAYS?

IT SAYS HIS NAME IS CHARLEY BUTTERS. I GUESS HE WAS A PAINTER.
OKAY... PROCEED GOOD, SIR.

TOLD ME I HAD A "BOLD VOICE". HE HAD ALL KINDS OF PLANS FOR ME. I WAS SHOCKED!

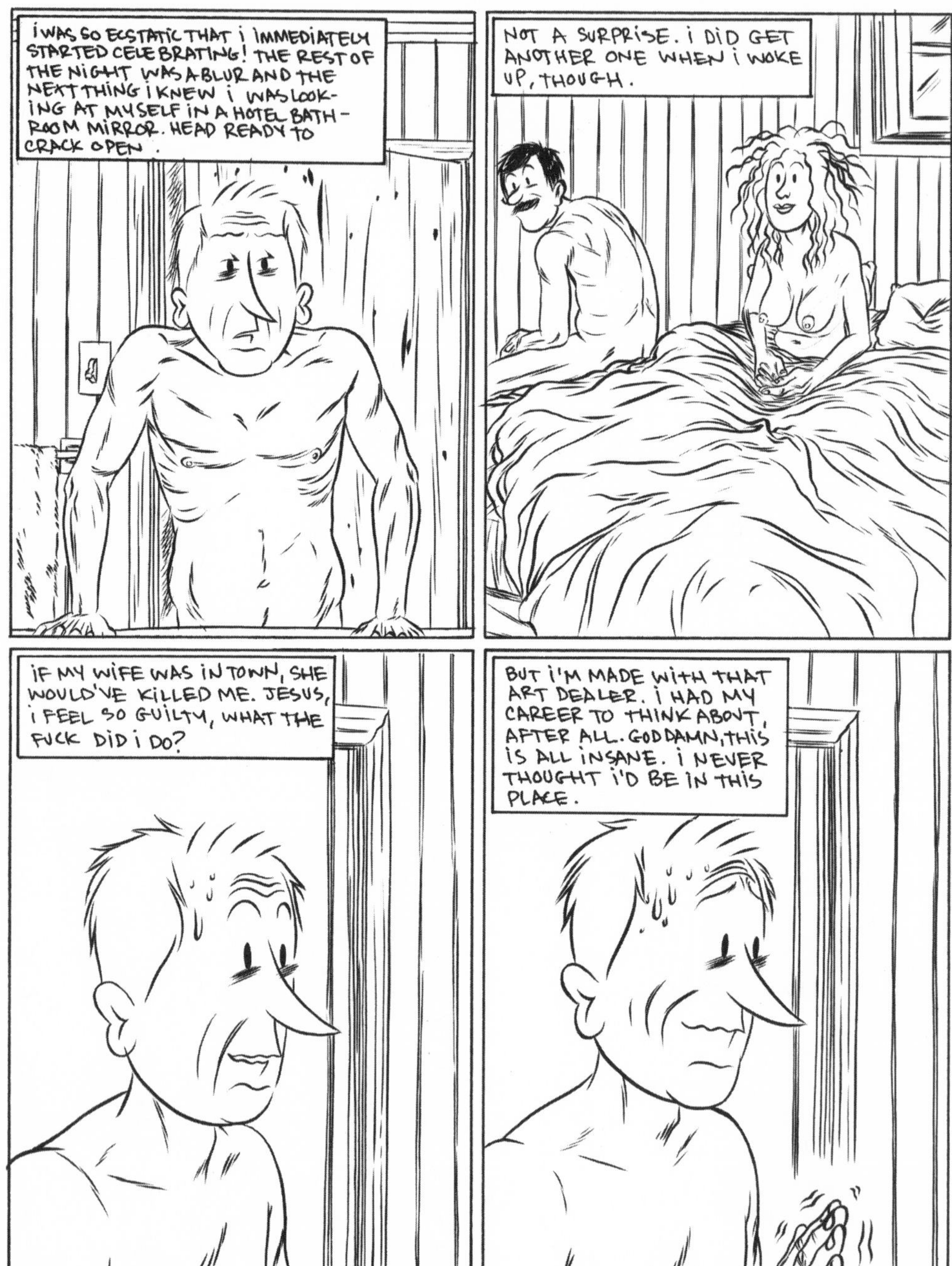
i WAS SO ECSTATIC THAT i IMMEDIATELY STARTED CELEBRATING! THE REST OF THE NIGHT WAS A BLUR AND THE NEXT THING i KNEW i WAS LOOK-ING AT MYSELF iN A HOTEL BATH-ROOM MiRROR. HEAD READY TO CRACK OPEN.
NOT A SURPRiSE. i DiD GET ANOTHER ONE WHEN i WOKE UP, THOUGH.
iF MY WiFE WAS iN TOWN, SHE WOULD'VE KiLLED ME. JESUS, i FEEL SO GUiLTY, WHAT THE FUCK DiD i DO?
BUT i'M MADE WiTH THAT ART DEALER. i HAD MY CAREER TO THiNK ABOUT, AFTER ALL. GODDAMN, THiS iS ALL iNSANE. i NEVER THOUGHT i'D BE iN THiS PLACE.

JESUS CHRIST! HE HAD SOME FAG IN HIM, DIDN'T HE?
PFFT! SHOULDN'T YOU SATANISTS BE MORE ACCEPTING OF THE "FAGS" THEN?
WE ARE NOT GOING TO HAVE A RELIGIOUS DISCUSSION RIGHT NOW!
C'MON! THEY'RE CALLED AN ABOMINATION AREN'T THEY? YOU GUYS ARE ALL ABOUT THAT, RIGHT?
LOOK, EVEN BUDDHISTS THINK IT'S WRONG!
MAN, YOU RELIGIOUS TYPES ARE ALL THE SAME.
WHAT DO YOU WANT ME TO SAY, STUART?!
THAT YOU'RE FULL OF SHIT, MIKEY, YOU SATANIST, YOU!
OH-- REAL NICE!
I THINK THE REASON YOU DON'T WANT TO HAVE A RELIGIOUS DISCUSSION IS BECAUSE YOU DON'T KNOW WHAT YOU ARE TALKING ABOUT!
YEAH.
BE MORE LIKE RANDAL. HE'S NIHILISTIC AT LEAST. RANDAL, PLEASE KEEP READING.

UH-- WHERE WAS I?
SKIP PAST THE BORING ART DEALER STUFF, WOULDJA?
YEAH... AMONGST OTHER THINGS.
I WAS WORKING ON A NEW SET OF PAINTINGS AND HIT A WALL. I COULDN'T GET PAST ONE PART OF ONE PAINTING. THE MORE I THOUGHT ABOUT IT, THE MORE ANXIETY I GOT.
... I DON'T WANT TO SOUND ... CRAZY...

THE VOICE WAS CLEAR ENOUGH THAT I COULD RESPOND TO IT... AND IT WOULD ANSWER ME, TOO.

THE LACK OF CONTROL REALLY TERRIFIED ME.

ELEANOR CAUGHT ME TALKING TO MYSELF. NOT EVEN SURE HOW I COVERED MYSELF ON THAT ONE. LUCKY, I GUESS.

JUST BLEW IT OFF AS THINKING OUT LOUD.

IT WAS A GOOD ENOUGH COVER THAT IT GOT HER TO LEAVE.

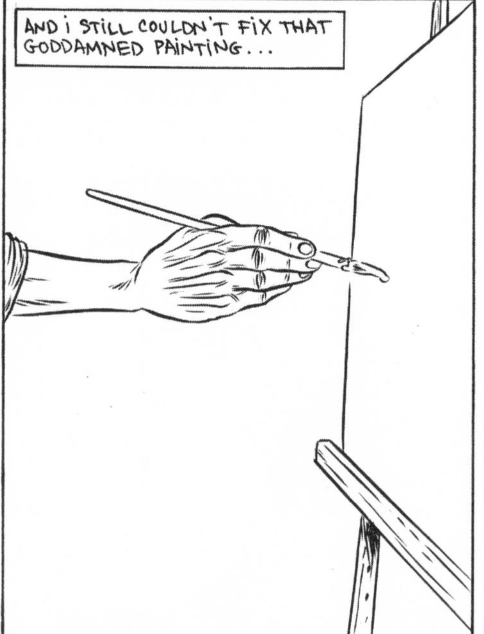
AND I STILL COULDN'T FIX THAT GODDAMNED PAINTING...

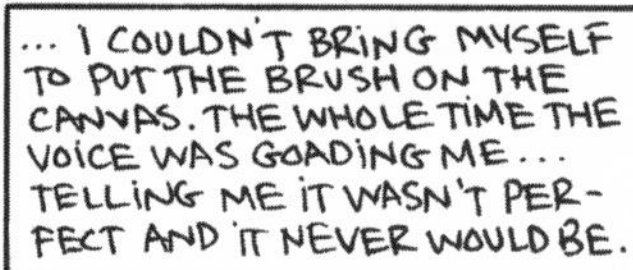
... I COULDN'T BRING MYSELF TO PUT THE BRUSH ON THE CANVAS. THE WHOLE TIME THE VOICE WAS GOADING ME... TELLING ME IT WASN'T PER-FECT AND IT NEVER WOULD BE.

MAN, WHAT A BASKET-CASE. PROBABLY SCHIZO AND DIDN'T EVEN REAL-IZE IT. SHAME.

RETARD.
YOU ARE A MORON, MIKE.

HE'S SCHIZO 'CAUSE HE'S GOT A WEAK MIND. PLAIN AND SIMPLE.

DO EVERYONE A FAVOUR AND NEVER SPEAK AGAIN. YOU ONLY EMBARRASS YOURSELF.
FOOL, FOOL, FOOL.

YOU GUYS ARE FUCKIN' DICKS.
WELL, YOU SAY SOME STUPID SHIT.
ALL OF YOU, SHUT UP!

I DON'T KNOW ABOUT YOU GUYS, BUT I'M BORED OF THIS.
YEAH, WE'RE BURNING DAYLIGHT HERE. JEEZ!
WAITWAITWAIT-AREN'T YOU GUYS A LITTLE BIT INTERESTED ABOUT WHAT HAPPENED TO THIS GUY?
NO, THE GUY WAS A SCHIZO HOMO. HE'S LONG DEAD AND WE'RE WASTING TIME CARING.
HAHA HA SEE?!!
I'M INTERESTED, FOR WHAT IT'S WORTH.
SIGH LET'S JUST GET THIS OVER WITH. I WOULD LIKE TO SEE SOME OF THE FOOTAGE YOU GOT, THOUGH.
WHATEVS, LET'S GO.

IT'S ONLY A COUPLE OF MINUTES OF FOOTAGE, BUT I'LL BURN IT ON A DISC FOR YOU.
THANKS, MAN.
... IT'S NOT JUST THE MAKE-UP... AND YOU ARE UPSET ABOUT SOMETHING.
WHAT? ... NO, I ...
WHAT?
I DON'T GIVE A SHIT ABOUT THIS VIDEO. I LIKE MAKING MUSIC, BUT HAVE YOU SEEN BLACK METAL VIDEOS BEFORE?
THEY ARE TERRIBLE.

BLACK METAL'S ALRIGHT, I GUESS, BUT I LIKE 60'S MUSIC. GARAGE ROCK... GIRL GROUPS.
HOW THE HELL DID YOU WIND UP SINGING IN A BLACK METAL BAND THEN?!
MIKE USED TO WORK AT THE RECORD SHOP I WORK AT AND WE WERE SCREWING AROUND ONE DAY. I THOUGHT I WAS MOCKING IT, BUT HE LOVED IT! HE ASKED ME TO START A BAND ... I THOUGHT IT WOULD BE FUN.
5$ CDS
5$ CDS
5$ CDS
IT'S NOT?
PFFT! IT'S ALL REGIMENTED. HE HAS A LIST OF BLACK METAL RULES POSTED IN OUR PRACTICE SPACE
OH MY GOD! WHAT ARE THEY?!
JUST WHAT'S GOING ON BACK THERE? ARE YOU GUYS PLANNING ON MURDERING, THEN BURYING US IN A SHALLOW GRAVE? FOR RAVENOUS ANIMALS TO EAT THE FLESH RIGHT OFF OUR ATTRACTIVE BONES?

SIGH

THE NEXT DAY...
HRM-AFTER SEVEN...
SIGH
DID YOU TELL THEM WE WERE CLOSING?
YEAH, 10 MINUTES AGO.
JESUS! WHAT IS THEIR PROBLEM?!
POSTERS $10
PLEASE... COME AGAIN.

ASSHOLES.

UH... HELLO?

MIKE? WAIT, WHAT?! YOU'RE CALLING FROM... OH MY GOD, I'M GOING TO FUCKING SMACK YOU!!
YEAH, I'M ON MY WAY.
JESUS CHRIST! IDIOT!
WHAT THE HELL IS WRONG?
THAT STUPID, FAT, STUPID IDIOT HAS BEEN ARRESTED!!
WHAT?! WHAT FOR?!
PUBLIC INDECENCY.
AW... GROSS!!!

GRMBL
TRAVIS!
WHUH?
HEY, KAT!
WHAT'S UP?
GOTTA BAIL MY FRIEND OUT OF JAIL. THE USUAL.
...OK!
WELL, I SHOULD SKEEDADDLE. MIKE'S GOING TO START SOBERING UP.
SURE, I WOULDN'T WANT TO BE SOBER ENOUGH TO REMEMBER I'M IN JAIL. YOU'RE FRIEND SOUNDS CHALLENGED.
HAHAHA HE IS! GOOD POINT!
HAHAHA

YOU-UH-WANNA GET A DRINK?
I'D LI
TRAVIS?!
I NEED YOUR KEYS TO LOCK UP.
ALRIGHT, ALRIGHT!
THANKS, MAN! SEE YOU LATER!
YEAH... NO PROBLEM.
DON'T YOU HAVE SOMETHING YOU SHOULD BE DOING?
SIIIGHH... YOU ARE RIGHT.
HAHAHA YEAH.
ANOTHER TIME! GOOD LUCK GETTING YOUR FRIEND OUT OF PRISON.
HAHAHA RIGHT... THANKS!

AND SO...
IT WAS UNJUSSTTT--
SIGH—LET'S JUST GET YOU TO THE CAR.
WHAT THE--?!
WHHUUUUHHHEEE
AAAAAAUUUUGGGHHHDAMMITT!!!

MOTHER FUCKER.

HRGH YOU FAT SHIT!

I HATE YOUR STUPID FUCKING FACE.

AND SO...
YEAH, IT TOOK THREE OF US TO GET HIM INTO THE BACKSEAT
HA HA HA
NOPE, STAYING IN TONIGHT. YEAH, NO, I'M DRIVING OUT TO THAT PAINTER'S CABIN TOMORROW. OK, BYE.
SSSIIIIIGGGHHHHHHH

SOON...
DING DONG

HHRRRRMMMMM

LATER, IDIOT.

THIS LOOKS LIKE THE PLACE
...I THINK.

...THEN AGAIN?

...MAYBE I'LL JUST EXPLORE A LITTLE FIRST.

...UUHHH...
WHEW GREAT!

I CAN'T TELL IF THIS IS FAMILIAR OR NOT!
HRM
WHAT A STUPID IDEA IT WAS COMING OUT HERE... AT NIGHT! SUCH A FUCKING IDIOT!

I HAD TO GET AWAY. THE CITY, THE PHONEY PEOPLE, THE DECA-DENCE... THE VOICES WERE GETTING WORSE AND KEEPING IT TOGETHER WAS GETTING HARDER.

SOME TIME TO MYSELF IN THE WOODS IS JUST WHAT I NEEDED.

EVENTUALLY, I FOUND A SPOT I COULD SETTLE IN. UNFORTUNATELY, I HAD NO TOOLS TO BUILD A CABIN.

I FIGURED IT OUT AND IT TOOK ME FOREVER TO GET IT ALL THERE.

AND SO...

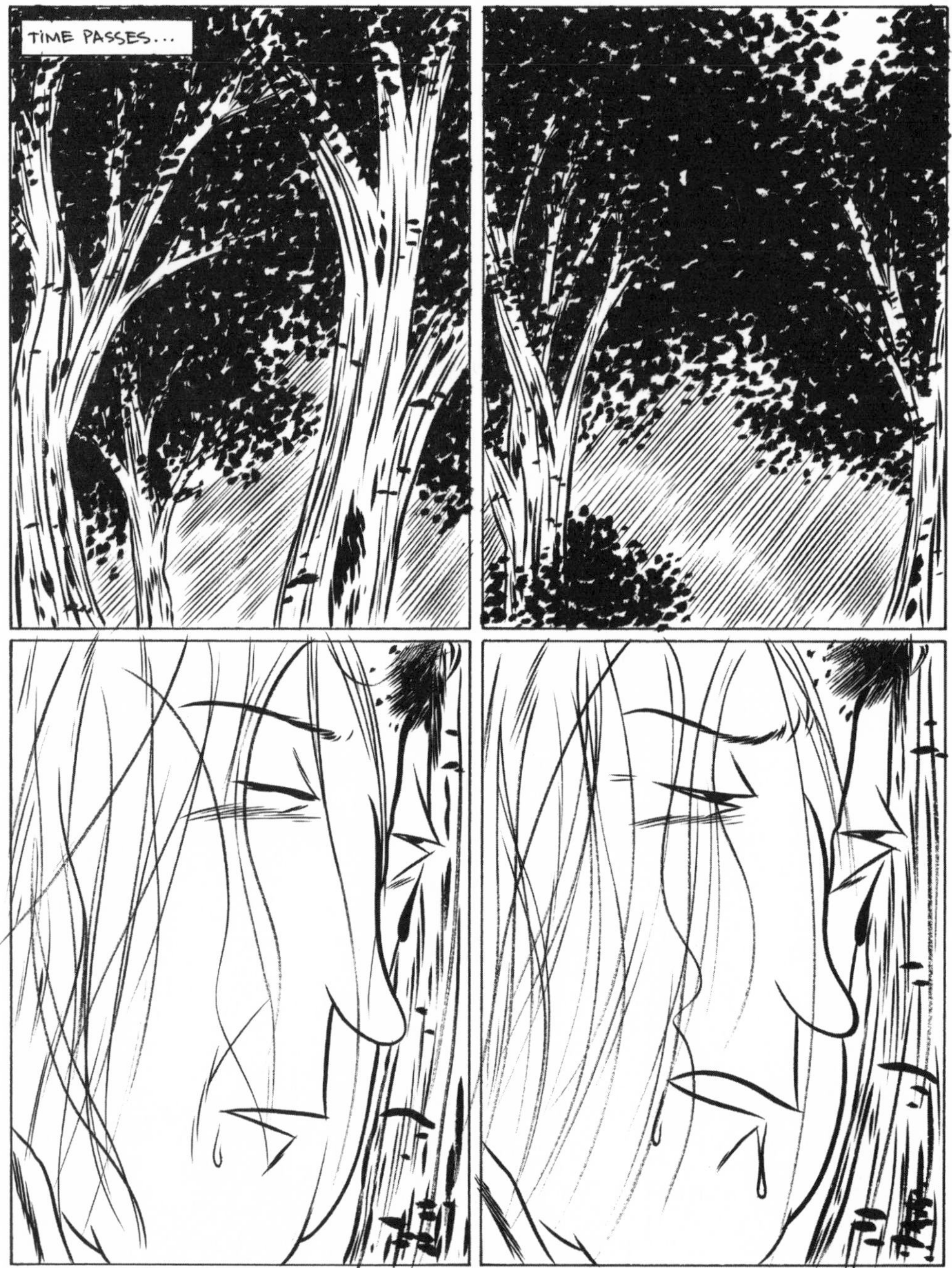
TIME PASSES...

NNGH

TNK
TNK
TNK
IDIOT
IDIOT
IDIOT !!!

OMIGODTHANKYOU

EVENTUALLY...

HOT DAMN!!!...

AND SO...

YA HAH!!

MEANWHILE...
CAN YOU BELIEVE HE JUST LEFT ME ON THE FRONT LAWN?! MY MOM LOST HER SHIT!!
≡SIGH≡ YOU ARE SUCH A CHILD. LET'S GO GET A DRINK, MIKE.
DON'T BE AN ASSHOLE, RANDY! YOU ARE SO FUCKING INSENSITIVE!
DRIiiiiiiNNK
FYI; THIS LIST IS COMPLETELY MORONIC. "BLACKMETAL RULEZ"? IDIOT.
ASSHOLE, I TAKE METAL TOTALLY SERIOUS, RANDY!
WE HAVE TO TAKE THIS SHIT "SERIOUSLY", MIKE! LEARN HOW TO SPEAK ENGLISH, GODDAMMIT!! AND, IT'S RANDAL!
WHO CARES, FUCK?!

HAVE IT YOUR WAY, I'M NOT WAITING ANY MORE. DRINK?
C'MON. RANDY?!

HOW MANY TIMES DO I HAVE TO TELL YOU MY NAME IS RANDAL?!?!

I'M SORRY, ALRIGHT?! JESUS!
WHY ARE YOU THROWING A TANTRUM? ARE YOU ACTUALLY PISSED OFF?
HE LEFT ME ON THE LAWN!!

WHAT ABOUT IT?
IT WAS REALLY HUMILIATING! PLUS, A DOG PEED ON ME!!
THAT IS PRETTY AMAZING, MAYBE IT WAS KARMA REARING HER UGLY HEAD?

COME ON, I'LL BUY YOU A DRINK.
THIS IS SO NOT COOL. TRAV IS SUCH A DICK.
HE BAILED YOU OUT OF JAIL, MIKE. HE WAS LOOKING OUT FOR YOU... TO A POINT.

THAT'S ANOTHER THING, WHY ARE YOU GUYS ALWAYS MAKING FUN OF ME?
REALLY? YOU WROTE OUT A LIST OF RULES, YOU PUT THOSE RULES UP ON THE WALL OF YOUR PARENTS BASEMENT, YOU SPELLED RULES WITH A 'Z' AND AN INVERTED CROSS IN THE WORD METAL!

YOU WOULDN'T MAKE FUN OF EITHER OF US FOR THAT?
PFFT!

DUDE, WE'RE NOT TWELVE YEARS OLD, JUST HAVE SOME FUN.
I'M TRYING TO, BUT YOU GUYS ARE--
TRYING TO HAVE FUN. I KNOW.

PFFT... "TRYING TO HAVE FUN" MY ASS. BASTARDS DON'T GIVE A FUCK.
BEER TIME.

AND SO...
PANT PANT PANT PANT

DAYS LATER...
BRRT
BRRT
BRRT
TRAVIS, I'M READY IF YOU WANT TO COME OVER AND START ON THIS EDITING.
WHAT?! TRAVIS?
TRAVIS?! IT'S STUART!
I HAVEN'T SLEPT IN DAYS. I'M OVER... CAFFEINATED.
WHAT IS YOUR PROBLEM?
IT'S THAT ARTIST, CHARLEY BUTTERS.
WHAT?

WHAT'S HE SAYING?!
I CAN'T UNDERSTAND YOU. JUST TELL ME
TELL HIM TO GET HIS ASS OVER HERE!!

SHUT UP!! I'M TRYING TO TALK ON THE PHONE!
WHO CARES?! TELL HIM WE'RE WAITING ON HIM, AS USUAL!
SHUT UP!!

HURRY UP, MIKE'S TREADING ON MY LAST NERVE.
STUART'S RIGHT, YOU'RE BEING VERY IRRITATING.

FUCK YOU! WHY AM I THE ONLY ONE THIS MATTERS TO?!
MIKE, YOU'RE TAKING THIS WAY TOO DAMNED SERIOUSLY.

THIS IS SERIOUS!!
YOU'VE REMADE "CALL OF THE WINTERMOON" BY IMMORTAL. I MEAN, COME ON!
YOU WERE TOTALLY INTO IT WHILE WE WERE FILMING!!
I WAS HAVING FUN, BUT THAT DOESN'T TAKE AWAY FROM THE FACT IT IS COMPLETELY RIDICULOUS.

YOU HAVE NO IDEA HOW ANNOYING YOU ARE, DO YOU? PLEASE SHUT UP.
YOU CAN'T--
SHUT UP!!!

MEANWHILE...
STREETTCCHH
HHRRGHH

ALRIGHT TRAVIS, PLAY NICE... HE'S STUPID AND DOESN'T KNOW ANY BETTER.

NO SMOKING!
RIGHT.
PAP

HEY. TRAVIS.
NICE OF YOU TO SHOW UP, TRAVIS. CHRIST! WE'VE BEEN WAITING FOR FUCKIN' EVER!
SIGH
ALRIGHT, NOW THAT WE ARE ALL HERE, LET US GET THIS OVER WITH.
I MEAN, SHOW US A LITTLE RESPECT, TRAVIS! YOU KEEP US ALL HERE
JESUS CHRIST, MIKE!
YOU'RE ALWAYS RUNNING YOUR DAMNED MOUTH!
ALWAYS CHIRPING AWAY, BEING THE MOST IRRITATING, VAPID PERSON IN THE ROOM. YOU GIVE METAL HEADS A BAD NAME.
FUCK YOU, ASSHOLE!
REALLY? THAT'S WHAT YOU GOT FOR ME?!
YEAH, THAT'S WHAT I GOT FOR YOU!
GUYS... RELAX. LET'S JUST GET THIS OVER WITH.

QUIT BEING SUCH A DICK, TRAVIS. ALWAYS GOTTA BE IN CONTROL. NEVER HAVE ANY FUN.
WAIT, WHAT?!
SIGH... BORED.
YEAH! YOU LOOK DOWN ON ME. THAT'S WHY YOU LEFT ME ON MY LAWN PASSED OUT!

YOU'RE NOT A FRIEND!
EXCUSE ME?! NOT A FRIEND?!
THAT'S RIGHT!
NOT ONLY DID I PAY TO GET YOU OUT OF JAIL, BUT I HAD TO DRAG YOU, BY MYSELF, TO MY CAR AFTER YOU PASSED OUT ON THE STREET!

I COULDN'T DRAG YOUR FAT ASS TO YOUR FRONT DOOR! NOT THAT IT WOULD'VE MATTERED, BECAUSE THERE WAS NO ONE TO LET YOU IN!
"FAT ASS"?!
YEAH!!

SO, WHAT, WAS I SUPPOSED TO STOP EVERYTHING I HAD TO DO BECAUSE YOU'RE A COMPLETE ASSHOLE?! WASN'T GOING TO SIT--
YOU'RE A SHITTY FRIEND, JUST ACCEPT IT.

FINALLY HE ADMITS IT! GODDAMN SELFISH PIECE OF SHIT!
RIGHT, I'M THE BAD FRIEND!
YOU ARE A TERRIBLE PERSON, MIKE. I'M DONE WITH YOU.

I AM FUCKING DONE.

I--

DID HE JUST QUIT THE BAND?!

WHAT THE FUCK IS WRONG WITH EVERYBODY?!
YOU.
NOW GET THE HELL OUTTA MY HOUSE!!
BUT, THE VIDEO?!
SHUT UP, MAN!
JUST SHUT THE HELL UP.
NOW GET OUT!

I MIGHT CONSIDER THIS DAY TO BE PERFECT. SOMETHING I THINK A LOT THESE DAYS.
NO NOISE. NO PEOPLE. JUST ME AND MY THOUGHTS.
... WHICH REMAIN SINGULAR.

EVEN THOUGH I WAS SURROUNDED BY PEOPLE ALL THE TIME, I FELT COMPLETELY ALONE... IN A WAY.

VOICES ASIDE... OBVIOUSLY.

AT LEAST I'M NOT ENTIRELY ALONE OUT HERE.

YUP. FEELIN' FINE.

DAYS LATER...
X-RAY RECORDS
GRMBL
HEY STUART, WHAT CAN I DO FOR YOU?
WHAT... REALLY?
I HAD SOMETHING I WANTED TO RUN BY YOU TODAY. YOU FREE IN A FEW HOURS. I'LL BRING YOU COFFEE.
UM... YEAH. I'M AT THE RECORD SHOP ALL DAY.
ALRIGHT, SEE YOU THEN.

SMASH
SIGH

HAIR DRESSER
HAIR DRESSER

AND SO . . .
WOW, IT'S BEEN A WHILE SINCE YOU'VE HAD A HAIRCUT, HASN'T IT?
YOU COULD SAY THAT.
SO, WHY ARE YOU CUTTING IT OFF NOW?
MAY I ASK WHY?
SURE.
TIME FOR A CHANGE!
BEFORE YOU GET STARTED... LAST CHANCE.
CUT AWAY.
ALRIGHT. LAY IT ON ME.

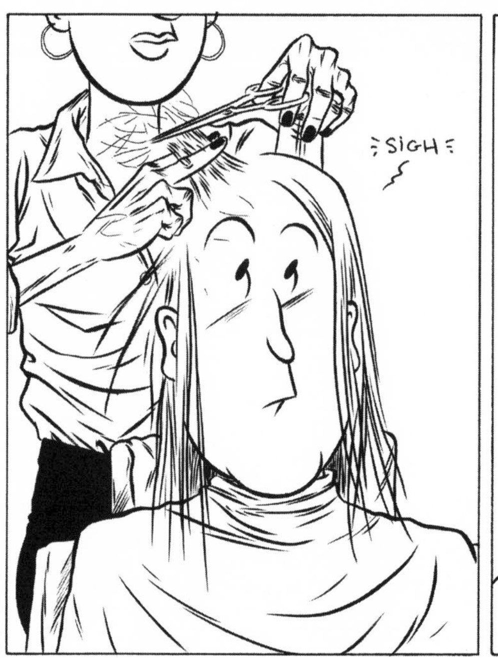
SIGH

MY OLDEST FRIEND IS BASICALLY RETARDED AND I MAY BE DONE WITH HIM. THIS HAIRCUT IS THE FIRST STEP TO ALL OF MY DREAMS COMING TRUE.

"DONE WITH HIM"?
Y'KNOW, BREAKING UP WITH HIM.
AH, I SEE.

AND SO...
WOW, I SHOULD'VE DONE THIS AGES AGO!
NO DUH.
THANKS AGAIN!
YEAH, OKAY.
TRA-LA-LA
SKIP SKOP SKEE

HEY! SO BEAUTIFUL!
MISS AMERICA!

WHY'D YOU FINALLY CUT OFF YOUR LONG, LUXURIOUS LOCKS, TRAVIS?
IT WAS JUST TIME.
GOOD EXCUSE TO FINALLY STOP LOOKING LIKE A GIRL.

WHAT?

I CAN SEE YOUR MOOSE KNUCKLE.
HAHAHA OH MY GOD, WHAT ARE YOU TRYING TO PROVE!
AGAIN... WHAT?

I THINK HE'S WEARING GIRLS JEANS!
SHUT UP!!!
HE DEFINITELY IS!
LOOK AT THE DETAILING ON THE FANNY.
WAHAHAHAHAHAHA
YOU TWO ASSHOLES HAVE NO IDEA WHAT YOU'RE TALKING ABOUT!
AND NEITHER OF YOU SHOULD BE TALKING TO ME ABOUT FASHION!
AWWW SOUR GRAPES. JOE COCKER WORE PURPLE BOOTS WITH MOONS AND STARS ON THEM!
YEAH, YOU'RE IN GOOD COMPANY!
YOU GUYS ARE A COUPLE OF REAL GARBAGE FACES.
I'M GONNA HEAD OUT.
WHAT?! COME ON! I WAS JUST GOING TO START COMPARING HIM TO EARLY BOWIE!
I'M GOING ON A COFFEE RUN. WHO NEEDS ONE?
YES, PLEASE! YOU KNOW HOW I TAKE IT.
PFFT!
JOHN?
...AMERICANO, PLEASE.

HEY KAT!
HEY!
OH MY GOD, YOU LOOK SO GOOD!
WHY THANK YOU, BEAUTIFUL KAT.
AHUH HUH HUH

SO, HOW ABOUT THAT DRINK TONIGHT?
UM-YEAH, OK!

EIGHT O'CLOCK AT THE CLOAK AND DAGGER?
THAT SOUNDS GREAT, I'LL SEE YOU THERE.

OK... SEE YOU THEN!
BYE!

THMP

HEH HEH

LATER...
TRAVIS.
STUART. WHAT'S HAPPENING, BABY?
YOU THINK I COULD BORROW YOUR BUTTERS DIARIES?
WHY DO YOU WANT THOSE?
I WAS-UH-THINKING OF MAKING A DOCU-MENTARY ON HIM.
REALLY?! YOU'VE GOTTA LET ME HELP! I KNOW EVERYTHING!
I DUNNO, TRAVIS...
C'MON, STUART!
GGRROOOANNNN WHAT CAN YOU OFFER ME?
I'M A REAL GO GETTER! I KNOW ALL ABOUT THIS GUY... YOU KNOW, A REAL-UH-EXPERT!
HRMM

ALRIGHT... YOU CAN BE SOME KIND OF... UH... CONSULTANT.
YOU NEED A TRUE BEAUTY! SOMEONE WITH A KIND OF ENCYCLOPEDIC KNOWLEDGE OF THE PAINTER. I'M GREAT WITH PEOPLE--
--WAIT, WAIT--
...THAT'S NOT A BAD IDEA, ACTUALLY. YOU ARE GOOD WITH PEOPLE, AND TOTALLY UNTHREATENING.
YES!! YOU WON'T REGR--
DON'T!!
DON'T SAY IT! THOSE WORDS LEAVE YOUR LIPS AND IT'S ONLY, WELL... REGRET.
FAIR ENOUGH.
COME TO MY PLACE LATER AND I'LL GIVE YOU THE DIARIES.
PERFECT.
SAY, WHAT IS IT WITH THIS BUTTERS GUY, ANYWAY?
I-UH-DUNNO.
HEH

HAD A BIT OF A SCARE TODAY. JUST HAVE TO STAY CALM AND THINK ABOUT MY OPTIONS.
CAN'T STAY HERE, THOUGH.

I WANT TO BE LEFT ALONE.

I CAN'T WATCH THIS. I CAN'T THINK ABOUT THE BAFFOONS DISSECTING MY LIFE. WHY I'M OUT HERE. WHY I LEFT.

NOW I'VE GOT TO MOVE MY WHOLE GODDAMNED LIFE AGAIN.

HELLO.
HEY!
BAR
WOW. YOU LOOKGREAT!
THANKS.
BAR
YOU CLEAN UP GOOD.

YEAH MAN, THAT WAS A KICKASS JAM, BRO!
WAAOOWN

OH... DID WE INTERRUPT YOU N=HIC=ECKING?
BAHAHA

I DON'T KNOW IF YOU TWO ARE AWARE, BUT ZEP *HIC* IS THE GREATEST BAND OF ALL TIME.
YEH
AN' I DON'T EVEN CARE THAT ROBERT PLANT SANG *HIC* ABOUT THE LORD OF THE FUCKIN' RINGS *HIC* LOTSA BANDS SING ABOUT THE LORD OF THE RINGS.
SO, Y'KNOW, IT'S PRETTY COOL. I COULD TOTALLY LIVE IN THE SHIRE. SWEET LIVIN', AM I RIGHT?
WHAAAAATT?
I-UH--
THEN WHEN PAGE RIPS INTO A SOLO LIKE - DEE DUN NUH NEEDER NOW - WOW WOW NUH NUNNAN BOODILY WOW!!
YEAH!

WEENILY NEENILY NEENILY NEENILY NEENILY WOOW-OW-OW-OW-OW-OW-OW
YEAH!! BURN IT UP! IT'S LIKE TREE BEARD'S HERE WITH US!
ALRIGHT... WELL... YOU GUYS HAVE A GREAT NIGHT.
OOOOHHH, I'M SO SORRY WE INVADED YOUR SPACE!
I KNOW =HIC= YOU TWO WERE NECKING!

LET'S GET OUT OF HERE.
WHERE DO YOU WANT TO GO?

OK, WE REALLY HAVE TO GO NOW!!

AND SO...

FUCK YOU!!!

WAARRGGHHH!!!

YOU'RE SUCH A DIRTY FUCKER, TRAVIS!!
YOU DIRTY BUTTHOLE!!

ALWAYS MAKIN' FUNNA ME!! ALWAYS MAKIN' OL' MIKE FEEL LIKE A FOOL!! SO TYPICAL!!

SHUT UP, YA DILDO! IT'S THREE IN THE FREAKIN' MORNIN'!

MIND YOUR OWN BUSINESS, DICK!
WHUH?! DID YOU JUST CALL ME A 'DICK'?!
YOU'D BETTER BELIEVE IT!
~ FUCKIN' ASSHOLE ~
YOU DON'T WANNA MESS WITH ME, MAN. REALLY.
FUUU-UUUCK YOU!!
EAT GARBAGE, GARBAGE FACE!!!

BWAGH!!

FUUU-UUCK YOU!!!

FUCKER!!!

RRRRRRRRRRRR
RRR RRR
RRR
RRRRR
RRRRRRR
RRR RRRR
RRRRR

MORNING, BEAUTIFUL.
MORNIN'!
SAY, WHAT TIME IS IT?

ABOUT A QUARTER TO ELEVEN.
SHIT! I'VE GOTTA BE AT WORK.
CAN I ASK YOU SOMETHING?
OF COURSE.
YOU TALKED ABOUT THIS PAINTER A LOT LAST NIGHT...
YEAH...?
WHY DO YOU CARE ABOUT HIM?
HMM... I-UH-HMM... WELL, I CAN'T FIGURE HIM OUT. I GUESS THAT'S WHY?

WHY ARE THEY AFTER ME? WHY CAN'T THEY LEAVE ME THE FUCK ALONE?
I CAN'T MAKE IT STOP.
HOPEFULLY THEY'RE GONE FOR GOOD.

WEEKS PASS...
COME ON, IDIOT!
IDIOT! HURRY UP!
YOU'VE GOT THIRTY SECONDS, STUPID IDIOT.
HAHAHA LOOK AT THIS! I GIVE STUART THIRTY SECONDS BEFORE HE STARTS YELLING AND HONKING HIS HORN!
232

WHAT A PSYCHO!

I SEE YOU BOZO'S UP THERE!!!

COME ON!!!!

OH MY GOD, WHY ARE YOU ALIVE?!
BAHAHAHA

WELL, I SHOULD GET GOING BEFORE HE DRIVES HIS TRUCK INTO THE SIDE OF YOUR BUILDING.
GOOD LUCK WITH THE INTERVIEW TODAY HANDSOME.

NOW GET OUTTA HERE!
OW

ALRIGHT, ALRIGHT...
I'M COMING ALREADY.
ZZZ
DON'T EVEN THINK ABOUT SMOKING IN MY CAR, PAL!
I KNOW THE DRILL, STUART.
THIS IS EXCITING!
YOU'RE RIGHT ABOUT THAT!
I HAVE NO IDEA WHAT I'M DOING.
YOU'LL BE FINE.

WHAT DO I DO? YOU KNOW ALL ABOUT THIS STUFF!
QUIT BEING SO FEMININE ABOUT THIS. JUST ACT NATURAL!
HEH. HOW HARD COULD IT BE?

WE'LL BE THERE IN A FEW MIN-UTES! YOU ALL SET? YOU PUMPED?
PULL OVER! I NEED A SMOKE OR TEN BEFORE WE GO IN THERE!!
SIGH
HURRY UP!!

AND SO...

THANK YOU SO MUCH FOR TALKING WITH US ABOUT CHARLEY.
YOU'RE WELCOME. HOW DID YOU KNOW ABOUT CHARLEY AND HIS PAINTINGS?
STUART AND I STUMBLED UPON HIS CABIN IN THE WOODS. WE FOUND DOZENS OF HIS DIARIES AND HUNDREDS OF THE -UH- SAME PAINTING.
... DIARIES? WAIT, HE WAS LIVING IN THE WOODS?
HAVE YOU SEEN HIM?! IS HE ALIVE?!
I'M SORRY, I DON'T KNOW. THE CABIN HAD BEEN ABAN-DONED FOR QUITE SOME TIME.

WE GOT SOME FOOTAGE OF THE CABIN... WE CAN SHOW IT TO YOU IF YOU'D LIKE?
OH... MAYBE LATER.
SO, WHAT CAN YOU TELL US ABOUT CHARLEY? THE KIND OF MAN HE WAS... WE GOT AN IDEA FROM THE DIARIES, BUT A LOT OF THAT SEEMS TO BE WHEN HE WAS -UH--
--TOUCHED?
UH-RIGHT.
OBVIOUSLY, HE WAS A WONDERFUL MAN FOR THE FIRST FEW YEARS OF OUR MARRIAGE.
SOMETHING CHANGED?
YES, HE BECAME DISTANT, WITHDRAWN... WE USED TO GO CAMPING WITH FRIENDS, WE'D GO DANCING... WE'D HAVE PARTIES ALL THE TIME--
DO YOU HAVE CHILDREN? UM- IF YOU DON'T MIND ME ASKING, THAT IS?

CHARLEY WAS UNABLE TO GIVE ME CHILDREN AND THAT'S ALL WE'LL BE SPEAKING ON THAT MATTER.
ANY HOW... AS I WAS SAYING BEFORE, HE WAS WONDERFUL. HE CHANGED, THOUGH. HE STARTED TALKING TO HIMSELF--
WHEN DID THAT START?
TCH
PLEASE, LET ME FINISH!
OH, I'M SORRY.
WHEN IT STARTED HE WOULD HIDE IT, BUT I CAUGHT HIM A FEW TIMES.
SIGH

-- WHY ARE YOU HERE? WHY DO YOU CARE ABOUT WHAT HAPPENED TO CHARLEY?
...I'M SORRY?
CHARLEY'S DISAPPEARANCE WAS NO MYSTERY. HIS MENTAL STATE WAS WORSENING BY THE WEEK AND HE COULD NOT KEEP A LID ON IT.
WHAT DO YOU MEAN?
HE BECAME A CONSTANT EMBARRASSMENT TO ME. RAMBLING IN PUBLIC! SCREAMING FITS... IT WAS AWFUL.
WHY DIDN'T YOU GET HIM SOME HELP?
YOU DON'T KNOW ANYTHING ABOUT IT, KID! YOU DIDN'T KNOW HIM, SO DON'T YOU DARE INSULT ME!
I TRIED. HE REFUSED. HE TRIED TO CONVINCE ME IT WAS STRESS. TWO DAYS LATER HE WAS GONE.

LOOK, I THINK IT WAS A MISTAKE TO DO THIS INTERVIEW.
NO NO NO!! LET'S JUST TAKE A BREAK! WE CAN START OVER AGAIN A LITTLE LATER!
SON, I APPRECIATE WHAT YOU'RE TRYING TO DO HERE, BUT I'VE LET ALL OF THOSE MEMORIES OF CHARLEY DIE.
I UNDERSTAND THIS MAY BE HARD BUT--
I'M SORRY!
WAIT! WHAT HAPPENED TO CHARLEY? DID HE EVER COME BACK?!
NO! AND THE INVESTIGATION WAS CALLED OFF AFTER TWO WEEKS.
TALK TO THE POLICE, TALK TO HIS FRIENDS, I DON'T CARE! I'M DONE WITH ALL OF THIS DIGGING UP OF THE PAST!
BUT, I HAVE SO MANY QUESTIONS!!

WOW... LESS THAN FORTY FIVE MINUTES AFTER WE ARRIVE AND THE MAIN INSIGHT INTO CHARLEY, THE FOCUS OF THE FUCKING DOC, KICKS US OUT OF HER GODDAMNED HOUSE. YOU ARE BAD AT THIS.
I DIDN'T EVEN HAVE A CHANCE TO GET INTO THE GOOD --
JUST SHUT UP... FUCKING IDIOT.
BUT --
39
I'M GOING TO THE CABIN TO GET SOME FOOTAGE TO MAKE SURE THIS DAY ISN'T A COMPLETE LOSS.
39
SIGH

40

~SIGH~

THE LIFE I KNEW IS GONE. THE MAN I WAS ... DEAD.
AND EVERY DAY I WAKE UP... IT'S FREEDOM.

part two
"the search"

ONE YEAR LATER . . .

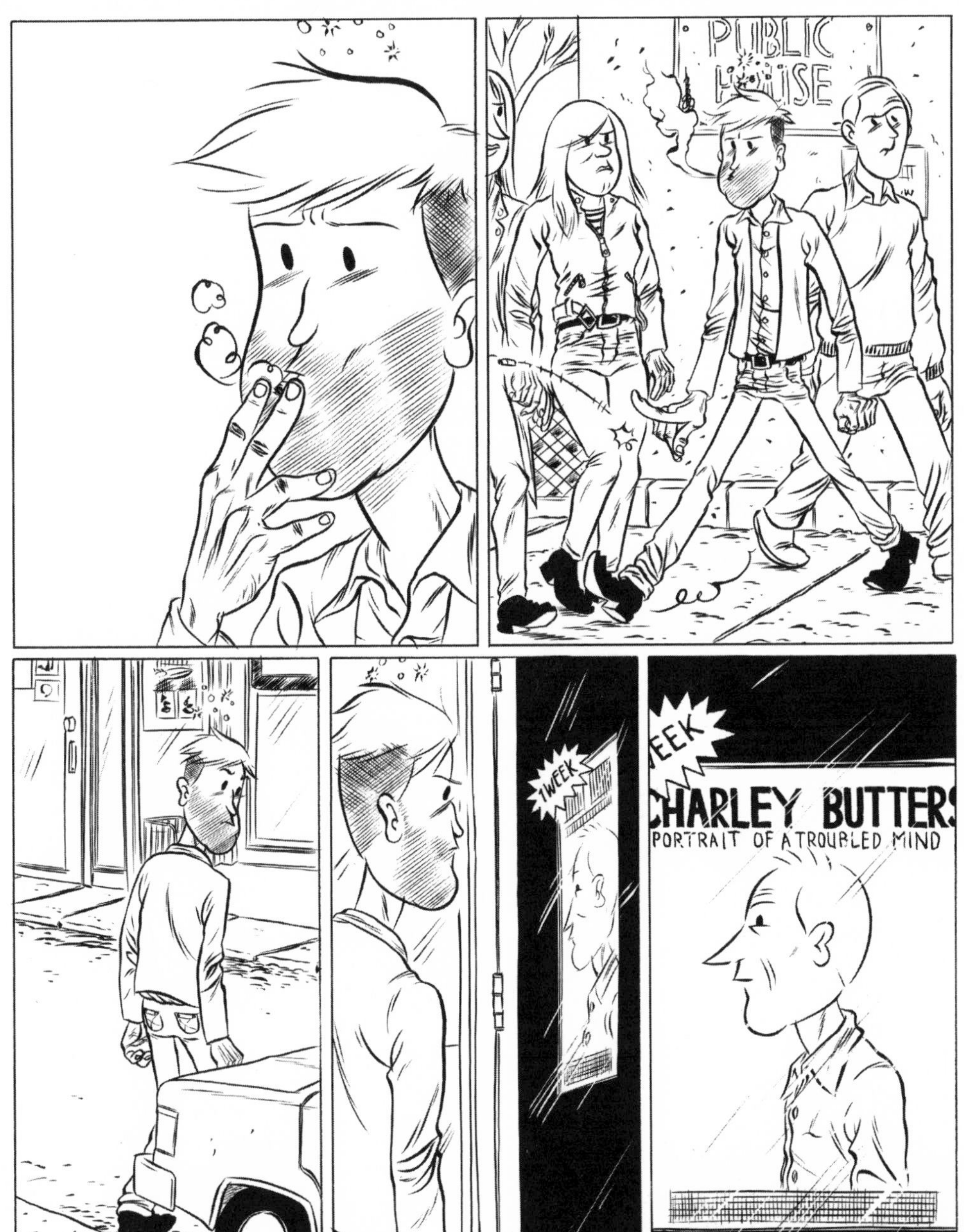
PUBLIC HOUSE
1WEEK
WEEK
CHARLEY BUTTERS
PORTRAIT OF A TROUBLED MIND

SPECIAL

YOU BELIEVE THIS SHIT? "PORTRAIT OF A TROUBLED MIND?" WHATTA TITLE!
UUUHHHH

Y'KNOW, THE GUY THAT MADE THIS MOVIE IS A REAL PIECE OF TRASH?! HE STOLE THE IDEA FROM ME!! CAN YOU BELIEVE IT???
UUHH, WE'RE JUST TRYING TO--

i INTRODUCED HIM TO CHARLEY BUTTERS! NOT LITERALLY, BUT IN A GENERAL SENSE. i FOUND HIS DIARIES IN AN ABANDONED SHACK IN THE WOODS, DAMMIT!
AL
LOOK MAN, THE MOVIE IS GOING TO START SOON.
HE KICKED ME OFF AFTER EVERYTHING i DID FOR HIM! HE DOESN'T CARE ABOUT CHARLEY'S LEGACY! NOT ONE FUCKING BIT!
SPECIAL
GET YOUR HANDS OFFA ME, MAN! CHRIST!
YOU ARE FUCKING CRAZY!
SPECIAL

HEY, WHAT CAN I GET YOU?
UUUUUMMM- -HMM--

I'LL HAVE A COUPLE BEERS, PLEASE.

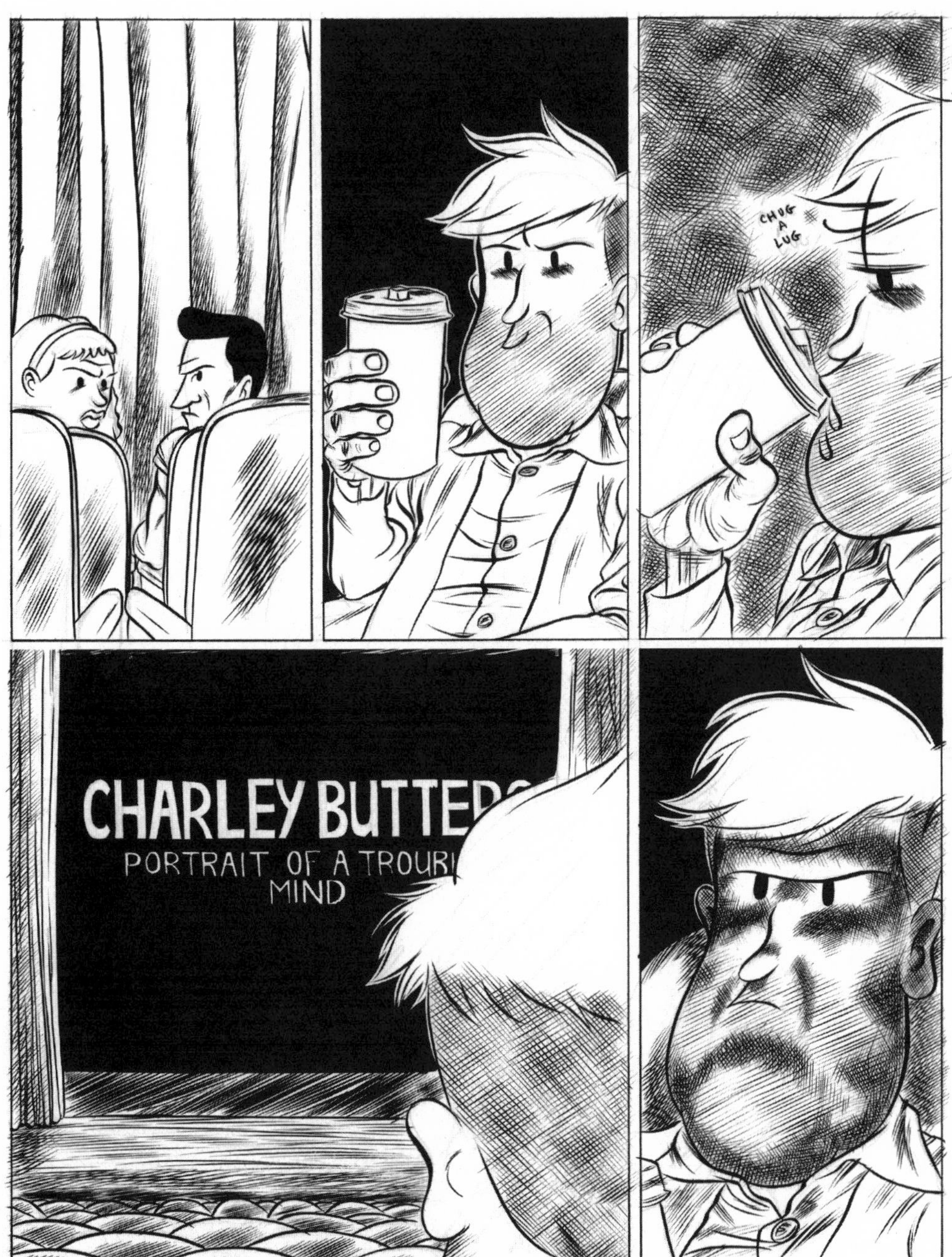
CHUG
A
LUG
CHARLEY BUTTER
PORTRAIT OF A TROUBL
MIND

AND SO...
TAY OUT!!!
GODDAMMIT LET GO OF ME!!
I'LL FUCKIN' SMASH YOUR FACE IN!!!
WHOA
WE DON'T WANT TO FIGHT YOU! WE JUST NEED YOU TO LEAVE.
YOU'RE CAUSING A DISTURBANCE!
HE STOLE THIS MOVIE FROM ME, DAMMIT!!
!!!

HELP ME!!

PORTRAIT OF A

PORTRAIT OF A
BRANG

PTOOO

HEY, GARBAGE FACES!
MY DAY JUST GOT A LITTLE BIT WORSE BECAUSE A COUPLE OF FUCKING FILM SCHOOL REJECTS WORKING A CON-CESSION STAND THREW ME OUT OF SOME HALF ASSED THEATRE. BRAVO.
I KNOW MY LIFE IS A FUCKING JOKE RIGHT NOW, BUT YOU TWO PROBABLY HAVEN'T ACCEPTED THAT YOURS ARE.
I JUST WANT YOU TO KNOW, THAT FEELING OF SUPERIORITY YOU HAVE RIGHT NOW WILL FADE. YOU'LL JUST BE A COUPLE OF IDIOTS SELLING POPCORN AND CANDY TO PRETENTIOUS ASSHOLES.
I'M GOING TO GO GET EVEN MORE DRUNK NOW, BUT I'LL BE BACK TO PISS ALL OVER YOUR DOORS. ENJOY!
CHNK
CHNK

CONVENIENCE
FFFUUUUCCCKKKK

BUAN
BUAN
BUAN
NNNNOOOOOOOOO
BUAN
BUAN
BUAN
BUAN
BUAN
BUAN
GET UP, I GOTTA GO TO WORK!
HRMMMMM
SMACK
SMACK

WHAT THE FUCK IS YOUR PROBLEM?

WHAT DID YOU SAY?
I WAS THINKING OUT LOUD.
...OK...?

SOON...
WELL, THAT WAS FUN!
SO, AM I GOING TO SEE YOU AGAIN, OR IS THIS...?
SURE, IF YOU WANT?

I MEAN, I'M KINDA BUSY, BUT--
UGH! TEXT ME IF YOU WANT. DON'T GIVE ME THOSE OLD CLICHES.
RIGHT

WHAT IS WRONG WITH YOU, TRAVIS?
POW

X-RAY
RECORDS

BLECH!
WHAT??
YOU LOOK TERRIBLE!

REAL NICE, DAVE! I'M HEART BROKEN AND MY LIFE IS A GIANT PILE OF SHIT. IT'S A TOILET! IT'S ALL A TOILET!
OH SPARE ME!

WHAT THE FUCK?? DON'T YOU CARE THAT I'M DYING INSIDE? DAVE??
VERY POETIC, TRAVIS. NOW GET TO WORK!

~UGH~ I HATE MY LIFE. I MISS HER. I'M ACTUALLY DYING.
I KNOW, PAL.
LOOK, WHY DON'T YOU TAKE THE WEEK OFF AND GET YOUR HEAD TOGETHER?
I CAN'T AFFORD IT, DAVE. I'VE BEEN DRINKING IT ALL AWAY RECENTLY.
I'LL LEND YOU SOME CASH, BUT I SWEAR TO GOD, IF YOU GO ON A BENDER AND SQUANDER MY GOOD WILL... I WILL FIRE YOU WITHOUT HESITATION.
REALLY?
YES. YOU REEK LIKE BOOZE ALL THE TIME AND YOU LOOK LIKE SHIT. GET IT TOGETHER, TRAVIS. FR'CRISSAKES.

DAVE, YOU ARE A SAINT!
YEAH, YEAH... I'LL GET THE OTHER GUYS TO COVER THE WEEK. YOU OWE ME BIG, THOUGH!
ANYTHING YOU WANT!

I WANT YOU TO WORK FOR ME THE WEEK YOU GET BACK. THE BANKING AND ALL THAT SHIT. NO QUESTIONS, OK?
YOU GOT IT.

I'M GOING FOR LUNCH, BE BACK IN 2 HOURS. THE ORDER IS HUGE THIS WEEK. HAVE FUN WITH IT!
UUUVVUHHH OK. HAVE A GOOD LUNCH.

AAAAAAAHHHHHHHH

DAYS LATER...
TRA LA LA

1574

WELL, ONE LI'L OL' DRINK WON'T HURT!
OPEN

STEVEN! HELLO!

OH JESUS.

DON'T WORRY! I'M NOT HERE TO VENT OR MAKE YOUR LIFE MISERABLE. TRUST ME.
I DON'T BELIEVE YOU, TRAVIS.
ola
I'M SERIOUS! I'M HEADING OUT OF TOWN FOR A WEEK TO GET MY HEAD STRAIGHT!
GOOD TO HEAR. WHAT BROUGHT THIS ON?
MY BOSS IS MAKING ME 'CAUSE I'M A STINKY, DRUNKEN BUM.
HA HA HA HA THAT'S RICH!
SO, I'M GOING TO GET MY SHIT TOGETHER!
WELL, I'M GLAD. I'LL MISS YOUR MONEY.
DROLL, STEVEN, DROLL. SET ME UP WITH ONE MORE FOR THE ROAD, THOUGH, GONNA RUN FOR A SMOKE.

I-UHHH-I- UMM-

... TRAVIS... I- UH-

OK- TIME TO GO.
BYE TRAVIS.

THAT FUCKIN' SUCKED.

EXIT

EXIT

YO. HIT ME AGAIN!

BWAN
BWAN
BWAN

GLP

HRK
HRK
HRK

GRGL
GRGL

AND SO...

GROAN

SLRPPP
FUCKIN' STUART.

AND SO...
SIGH... OKAY...

HRMM

MOTHER FUCKER BOUGHT A NEW JEEP.

KNOCK
KNOCK
KNOCK

TRAVIS?
WHAT ARE YOU DOING HERE? ALSO, YOU LOOK LIKE SHIT, IN CASE YOU WEREN'T AWARE.
LOOK STUART, I'M JUST HERE FOR THE DIARIES.
A:) FUCK YOU, AND B:) THEY'RE NOT YOUR FUCKIN' DIARIES!
LIKE HELL! I FOUND THEM, I LENT THEM TO YOU!
RIGHTFULLY, THEY ARE MRS. BUTTERS'!
THAT'S REALLY CONVENIENT, STUART. LIKE YOU GIVE TWO SHITS!
I DO, BECAUSE I'M A CONSCIENTIOUS PERSON LIVING IN THE WORLD. SHE NEEDED CLOSURE!
THAT IS FUCKIN' RICH!

YOU GIVE A SHIT NOW, BECAUSE YOU HAVE TO! IF IT WEREN'T FOR ME, NEITHER OF YOU WOULD KNOW A DAMN THING ABOUT CHARLEY! YOU WOULDN'T HAVE YOUR LITTLE INDIE FAVE OF A DOCUMENTARY AND NO ONE WOULD GIVE A WET FART ABOUT YOUR TWO BIT CAREER AS A VIDEOGRAPHER.

YOU NEED TO STEP THE FUCK BACK BEFORE I GET ANGRY.
GIVE ME THE MOTHERFUCKING DIARIES, STUART. I'M NOT PLAYING AROUND HERE.

GET THE FUCK AWAY FROM MY HOUSE, TRAVIS!
WHAT ARE YOU GOING TO DO IF I DON'T?
DON'T TEST ME!

GIMME THE FUCKIN' DIARIES, YOU UGLY ASSHOLE!

I'M ABOUT TO KICK YOUR TEETH IN!
YOU AND WHAT ARMY??
FFFF
BANG

MMPH
RRRRRAAAAHHFUCKERRRR
YOU ARE A FUCKING MANIAC!!!
FUCK YOU!!!
WHERE ARE THEY????

AH HA!!
Y'KNOW WHAT? FINE. TAKE THEM. YOU CLEARLY NEED THEM TO FILL SOME VOID IN YOUR LIFE.
YOU DON'T KNOW SHIT ABOUT MY LIFE.
YOU'RE RIGHT, I DON'T, BUT I DO KNOW YOU'RE JUST SOME SLUG SLITHERING THROUGH LIFE WITH VIRTUALLY NO PURPOSE.
WHAT THE FUCK?
I MEAN, LET'S FACE IT, YOU'RE NOT EXACTLY MAKING A SPLASH IN THE WORLD.
WHAT IS WRONG WITH YOU??

YOU, YOU'RE 37, YOU WORK IN A RECORD STORE, YOU STILL LIVE IN A CRAPPY APARTMENT--
JUST BECAUSE YOU THINK I SHOULD LIVE A CERTAIN WAY DOESN'T MEAN I'M A FUCKING SLUG, YOU ASSHOLE.
YEAH - LET'S NOT FORGET ABOUT HOW YOU GOT DUMPED BECAUSE YOU HAVE NOTHING TO OFFER, YOU LOSER. YOU'RE PATHETIC.
WHOA! STEP THE FUCK BACK!
WE WEREN'T EVEN TALKING WHEN THAT HAPPENED, SO HOW COULD YOU POSSIBLY HAVE ANY KNOWLEDGE OF THAT?
AND LET'S NOT POINT ANY FINGERS, STUART! YOU'RE AS BIG A PHONY AS ANYONE!!
OH?? ENLIGHTEN ME!
YOUR SHODDY DOC MADE ALMOST NO IMPACT ON THE "ART" WORLD, FUCKFACE! IT WAS BAD AT BEST. YOU COMPLETELY MISSED THE POINT, AND SPENT WAY TOO MUCH TIME FILMING SCENERY. NOTHING RESOLVED! IT WAS TOO SENTIMENTAL, AND YOU COMPLETELY JUMPED TO CONCLUSIONS! IT WOULD HAVE BEEN AN EXCELLENT DOC IF A FIRST YEAR FILM STUDENT MADE IT! FUCKING HACK!

YOU'VE PUT NOTHING INTO THE WORLD, YOU ADD NOTHING TO THE WORLD. YOU MAY AS WELL JUST JOIN CHARLEY IN THE WOODS, AND DISAPPEAR SO WE CAN FORGET ABOUT YOU...

...OR JUST DIE.

YEAH MUTHAFUCKAAAAHH

SKKKREEEEE

AND SO...
FUCK!

GET IT TOGETHER, TRAVIS! COME ON!

WHY DO YOU HAVE TO BE A SELFISH IDIOT ALL THE TIME??

COME ON!

STUART DOESN'T KNOW SHIT! FUCK HIM! FUCK MIKE! FUCK KAT! BUNCH OF ASSHOLES! GODDAMN JOKE OF A LIFE.!

CRYING NOW, HUH?

SIGH
BRRRIIIINGGG

HEY RANDALL, WHAT'S UP?

STUART CALLED ME AND TATTLED ON YOU.
THAT GUY IS A REAL PIECE OF SHIT.
WELL, HE'S CERTAINLY MAD AT YOU.
HE TOLD ME I SHOULD GO INTO THE WOODS AND DISAPPEAR.
YEAH, HE TOLD ME. I HAD TO GET IT OUT OF HIM, BUT HE TOLD ME. HE ALSO SAID THAT HE WAS GOING TO CALL THE COPS ON YOU FOR THEFT AND WRECKING THE LAWN.
THAT'S JUST WHAT I NEED! FUCKING JAIL TIME! MY LIFE IS OFFICIALLY A GODDAMN JOKE!
I TALKED HIM OUT OF IT, DON'T WORRY. NOTHING IS GOING TO HAPPEN.
HOW'S THAT?
I TOLD HIM YOU'D FIX HIS LAWN--
WHAT??
RELAX! I'LL HELP YOU! I ALSO TOLD HIM THAT IF HE CALLS THE COPS, I'D KICK HIS HEAD IN!
AWWW

YOU'D DO THAT FOR LITTLE OL' ME? YOU'RE A REAL PRINCE Y'KNOW THAT?
YOU DON'T HAVE TO GO ON THE LAM ANYMORE. HE'S NOT CALLING THE COPS, GIRL.
BRO'S BEFORE HO'S, MAN. YOU WANNA GRAB COFFEE SOME TIME THIS WEEK?
YEAH, BUT LATE IN THE WEEK. I'M HEADING OUT OF TOWN FOR A FEW DAYS.
DROLL.
ALRIGHT, YOU'LL COME OVER, I'LL MAKE LEMON SQUARES, YOU'LL KVETCH, I'LL VERY PATIENTLY LISTEN. WE'LL RAP, OKAY?
BETTY CROCKER OVER HERE.
ALRIGHT, I HAVE TO GET BACK TO WORK.
THANKS, PAL.
YOU GOT IT.

AAAAAAAHHHHHH
SIGH
GODDAMMIT

GENERAL No 12

OPEN
COME

OPEN

WE HAVE MAPS
HELLO THERE.
HELLO.
I WAS JUST LOOKING FOR A FEW THINGS FOR A LITTLE CAMPING TRIP...
TAP TAP
... UMM- WHAT ARE YOU LOOKING FOR EXACTLY?
SOME FOOD, CANDLES, OR A LANTERN, BEER, WHISKEY, THAT KIND OF THING.
THE GROCERY STORE HAS ALL THE LIQUOR YOU NEED. HOW MANY PEOPLE YOU BUYIN' FOR? WE DON'T WANT ANY ROWDY TYPES UP HERE!

OH, IT'S JUST ME. I'M LOOKING FOR SOME INFORMATION ON WHAT HAPPENED TO THIS PAINTER, CHARLEY BUTTERS. RING ANY BELLS? IT WOULD HAVE BEEN THE EARLY 60'S. WERE YOU AROUND THEN?
YEAH, WE WERE HERE... BUTTERS, EH? HMM - I DON'T THINK SO.
HAROLD?? YOU REMEMBER A GUY NAMED "BUTTERS" FROM 'ROUND HERE BACK IN THE 60'S? WE WAS KIDS!
WHATCHA HOLLERIN' FOR???
HIS NAME IS BUTTERS. HE WAS LIVING UP IN THE WOODS--
OH SHIT! THERE WAS A GUY CALLED BILL UP THERE AT THE TIME. STILL SEE HIM EVERY NOW AND AGAIN. REAL WEIRDO.
THERE WAS ANOTHER CRAZY SUMBITCH UP THERE FOR A WHILE.
REALLY???
YEAH, HE CAME AROUND FOR ABOUT A YEAR, BUT I HAD TO TELL HIM TO GET LOST. TALKING TO HIMSELF, SOME TIMES YELLING. BAD FOR BUSINESS, THAT GUY. MADE EVERYONE PRETTY UNEASY.

DID YOU TALK TO HIM?
I DON'T REMEMBER THIS GUY!
BAH!
HE WENT ON ABOUT BEING A PAINTER.
WOOLS SOCKS $3/PAIR
THAT CRAZY SHIT?! I THOUGHT HE WAS SOME GROUP OF SEVEN WANNABE!
WHO WAS THE OTHER GUY THEN?
OLD BILL!
STILL COMES AROUND FROM TIME TO TIME. BEEN UP HERE SINCE THE LATE 50'S. HE WAS A LITTLE OLDER THAN ME. HAVEN'T SEEN HIM FOR A WHILE. PROBABLY RODENT FOOD, IF YOU ASK ME!
I'VE GOTTA FIND THIS GUY!
GOOD LUCK, THIS GUY DOES NOT WANT TO BE FOUND. A REAL OFF THE GRID TYPE.
YOU BUYING ANYTHING?

COMEONIN
CAMPING GEAR
FOOD SUPPLIES
...BOOZE...

AND SO...
HOW THE HELL AM i SUPPOSED TO GET ALL THIS SHIT TO THE CABIN?

SOON...
HEH SMART!

CHUG CHUG

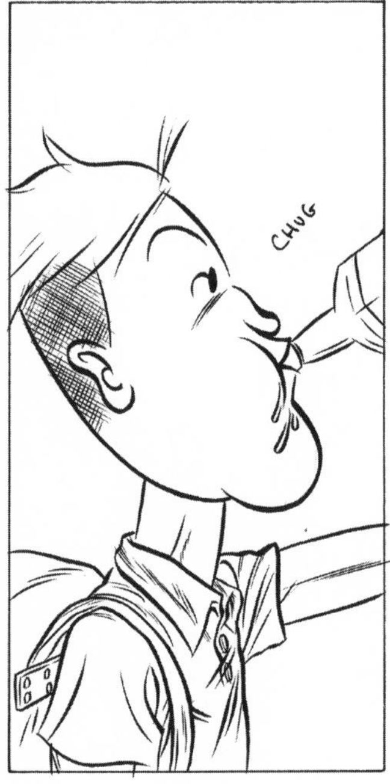
CHUG

FUCKIN' FINALLY...

SHIT... I WANT SOME FUCKIN' RAVIOLIS!
GRMBL

RAVIOLI
CHEF

I WANT THEM FUCKIN' RAVIOLIS!
AHA!
RAVIOLI
RAVIOLI CHEF, WHERE YOU BEEN ALL MY LIFE?
I LOVE YOU!

CHRUNCH
OBLIGED, KID.

LATER...

JESUS CHRIST!
WATER!!!

GLK
GLK
GLK
GLK

WHERE ARE MY CIGARETTES?
OH MY GOD... I'M DYING.
GOTTA BE SOME IN HERE.
OOOGHH

WHAT THE FUCK IS WRONG WITH ME? FUCK.

WHAT THE...?
THAT'S A BIG
FOOT PRINT, MAN.

UHHH

NAH...CAN'T BE.

WAS IT? ... COULD BE...

CAN'T BE CHARLEY. HOW COULD HE POSSIBLY STILL BE ALIVE?
THIS IS TOO FREAKY, MAN.
WAS IT THAT OTHER GUY? NAH--GOTTA BE A HIKER PASSING BY...?
THIS IS TOO FREAKY. JESUS CHRIST.
SHIT.
OR...OLD BILL IS STILL LURKING IN THESE WOODS?
SHIT, MAYBE CHARLEY IS STILL ALIVE!

AND SO...
RAVI

WHAT WAS REALLY GOING THROUGH YOUR HEAD, CHARLEY? I GET THAT YOU WERE FUCKED UP, I GET THAT YOU WERE WRACKED WITH GUILT OVER LEAVING YOUR WIFE, BUT...

...WHAT THE FUCK HAPPENED TO YOU?

WHY DO I HAVE ALL THESE QUESTIONS? IS SOMETHING COMPLETELY MISSING FROM MY LIFE THAT I NEED THIS MYSTERY TO SOLVE? WHY SHOULD I CARE ANYMORE? NOTHING GOOD HAS COME FROM YOUR PRESENCE IN MY LIFE, CHARLEY.

MAYBE YOU WERE SCHIZO AND NEVER DID ANYTHING ABOUT IT. MAYBE YOU WERE A COWARD. COULDN'T FACE YOURSELF? MAYBE THE VOICES WERE JUST YOUR FUCKING CONSCIENCE. MAYBE JUST A TOTAL ASSHOLE?

I HAVE NO IDEA! I HAVE NO IDEA WHY I HAVE TO KNOW! MAYBE I'M THE ONE WHO'S FUCKED IN THE HEAD?!

WHY DID YOU LEAVE?
WHY DID YOU LEAVE?
WHY DID YOU LEAVE, CHARLEY?

THESE DON'T TELL ME SHIT! WERE YOU JUST SOME GROUP OF SEVEN WANNABE LIVING OUT SOME FUCKING FANTASY???

WHO THE FUCK WERE YOU?

WHY THE FUCK DID YOU LEAVE???

SHE THOUGHT I WAS CRAZY FOR GETTING SO OBSESSED!! WHO THE FUCK IS SHE??? FUCKING NORMAL!!!

WHO THE FUCK IS SHE??? HUH, CHARLEY??!!
WHY THE FUCK DID SHE GO??? YOU!!!
YOU DROVE HER AWAY!!!

YOU DID IT!!! SHE LEFT BECAUSE OF YOU, YOU CRAZY MOTHER FUCKER!!!

HHF
HHF

HOLY SHIT!

OCT. 12, 1960
IT'S STARTING TO GET COLD OUT.
I'VE HAD IT EASY SO FAR, BUT I'M AFRAID I'M NOT PREPARED FOR WINTER.
GOD KNOWS IT GOES ON FOREVER IN CANADA, AND FROM WHAT I UNDERSTAND, AS A CITY SLICKER, COLD IN THE CITY IS A BREEZE COMPARED TO BEING OUT HERE.

I HAVE TO BUILD A NEW SHELTER BEFORE IT GETS TOO COLD. I CAN'T STAY HERE ANYMORE. PEOPLE ARE LOOKING FOR ME.
GOT NO MONEY, THOUGH. SPENT THE LAST OF IT ON A RIFLE.
GOOD THING I WENT HUNTING AS A YOUNG MAN, OR I'D BE IN TROUBLE.
I'D KILL FOR A CUP OF COFFEE. HAVEN'T HAD ONE IN WEEKS.

OCT. 14, 1960...
THOUGHT I'D NEVER SEE ANOTHER PERSON AGAIN. HAVEN'T SPOKEN A WORD TO ANOTHER HUMAN BEING IN, I DON'T KNOW HOW LONG.

TALK TO MYSELF A LOT THESE DAYS. CAN'T TELL IF I'M LOSING IT, OR ALREADY LOST IT.

DO I ACTUALLY HEAR VOICES ANYMORE OR AM I JUST SO ALONE OUT HERE THAT I'VE CREATED AN INTERNAL WORLD FOR MYSELF? I HAVE NO PERSPECTIVE ON THE MATTER ANYMORE.

SNAP
CRACKLE

I SAW A MAN TODAY. HE LOOKED LIKE HELL.

WE STAYED AWAY FROM EACH OTHER...

NOT SURE IF HE'S A THREAT OR NOT, OR WHERE HE'S LIVING FOR THAT MATTER. NOT WILLING TO FINDOUT AT THE MOMENT.
OCT 17, 1960...
DAMN, IT'S GETTING COLD OUT HERE. GOOD THING MY SHELTER IS COMING TOGETHER FAST. ANOTHER DAY OR SO, AND IT SHOULD BE DONE. CAN'T STAY OUT HERE.
NO STOVE, SO I'M NOT SURE IF I'LL ACTUALLY BE ABLE TO LAST IN THIS SHACK, BUT I CAN'T RISK ANYONE FINDING ME.

OCT. 19, 1960...

WHILE I WAS SKINNING A RABBIT TODAY, THAT MAN CAME UP TO ME. SAID HIS NAME WAS BILL.

OFFERED HELP IF I NEEDED IT.

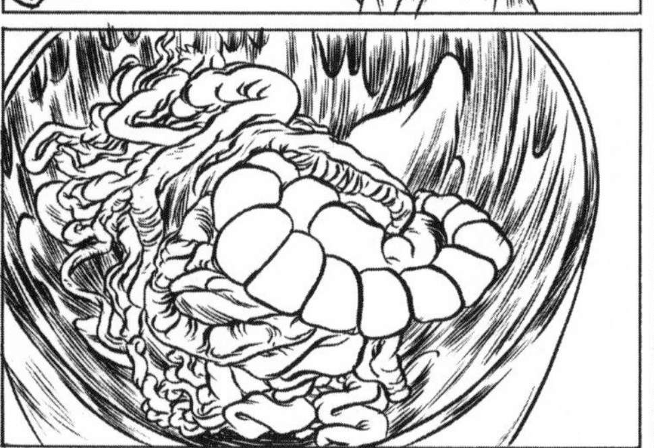

HE'S BEEN OUT HERE FOR ABOUT FIVE YEARS, JUST LIVING OFF THE LAND. I WAS PRETTY IMPRESSED BY HIM. STOIC AS HELL.

DOESN'T SEEM LIKE HE WANTS TO BE PALS OR ANYTHING... MORE NEIGHBOURLY, I SUPPOSE.

IT'S A BIT OF A STRANGE THING TO DO CONSIDERING HE CAME OUT HERE TO GET AWAY FROM PEOPLE. OH WELL. WHO AM I TO QUESTION?

I DO GET THE FEELING THAT HE WAS SIZING ME UP THE WHOLE TIME, THOUGH. NOT OVERLY FRIENDLY. KIND OF LOOKING AROUND A LOT. WHEN HE DID MAKE EYE CONTACT, IT WAS PIERCING.

NOT THE KIND OF GUY I WOULD WANT TO BE ON THE WRONG SIDE OF.

IT'S COLD AS HELL OUT HERE. I HAVE TO GO BACK TO THE OLD CABIN TO GET SUPPLIES SO I CAN PAINT, WHICH I DON'T DO ANYMORE. ALL I SEEM TO DO IS WRITE IN THESE GODDAMN BOOKS. WELL, NO MORE.

I'M NOT OUT HERE TO WRITE. IT'S TIME TO GET BACK ON THE HORSE AND PAINT.

SO, IF ANYONE EVER FINDS THIS, THIS IS MY FINAL ENTRY. I'M DEEPER IN THE WOODS WITH ONLY MY THOUGHTS AND SOME PAINT.

THESE LITTLE NOTEBOOKS ARE MY CANVAS NOW. MODERN LIFE IN THE CITY HOLDS NO INTEREST FOR ME ANYMORE.

GOOD BYE FOR NOW... SEE YOU IN THE NEXT LIFE... CHARLEY
FLP FLP FLP
THAT'S IT??
YOU DIDN'T ANSWER A SINGLE FUCKING QUESTION!!!

WARGH

AND SO...
FELLAS! I'M BACK!
HRM
ALRIGHT! I'M GOING FOR LUNCH! SEE YOU IN A COUPLE HOURS!

TELL ME ALL ABOUT IT WHEN I GET BACK.
GREAT. ENJOY IT.

I'M GETTING A COFFEE, MAN. THERE'S AN ORDER THAT NEEDS TO BE DEALT WITH.
TAKEN CARE OF.

HEY, THANKS FOR COVERING ME THESE LAST FEW DAYS.
IT'S COOL, PAL.

ANYTHING TO GET YOUR RANK BODY OUTTA HERE FOR A WEEK.

VERY FUNNY.

HEH.

AAAAAAAHHHHH

CLOSING TIME...

DUM

RANDALL. YOU BUSY?

OH OK... ALRIGHT... SURE... SEE YOU TOMORROW.

WELL, DRINKY TIME.
UM... YOU'D BETTER BRING ME ANOTHER ROUND. I'LL BE DONE WITH THESE IN A MINUTE.
...OK...
WOW, YOU WEREN'T KIDDING.
I'M THIRSTY TONIGHT.
ANOTHER?
JUST A BEER THISTIME.

THIS GUY LOOKS ROUGH.
...I'M GONNA SEE IF HE'S OKAY.

HEY BUDDY, HOW ABOUT i CALL YOU A CAB?
. . . . . .
HGK HGK

OH SHIT!!! YOU'RE NOT PUKING ARE YOU??

SOB BLUBBER
SHE SNRT LEFT ME
SOB SOB
OH CHRIST

I'M SO FUCKIN' MORTIFIED.
I'VE SEEN WORSE, PAL.
REGARDLESS... I'M SORRY.
NO WORRIES.
IT'S UNDIGNIFIED!!! LIKE RUNNING FOR PUBLIC TRANSIT!!! OR WHITE PEOPLE DANCING!!!
OK! TAKE HIM HOME!!!
WILL I EVER SEE YOU AGAIN?
WITH MY LUCK, YES.
OK, PERFECT!
SEE YOU TOMORROW!!
FUCKIN' CHRIST

NO SURPRISE HERE...

TRAVIS. YOU LOOK TERRIBLE.
THAT'S RUDE, Y'KNOW.

WHAT'S GOING ON? I HAVEN'T SEEN YOU IN AGES.
...
WHAT?

UGH, I HATE TALKING ABOUT THIS.
HEY, WHAT CAN I GET YOU?
JUST COFFEE, PLEASE.

... SHE DUMPED ME. I GOT DUMPED.
JESUS, I'M SORRY TO HEAR THAT. WHY THOUGH? YOU TWO SEEMED HAPPY ENOUGH.
I THOUGHT SO TOO!

IT GOT TO A POINT WHERE SHE THOUGHT I WAS WASTING MY TIME WITH ALL THIS BUTTERS STUFF. ESPECIALLY AFTER STUART KICKED ME OFF THE FILM. THEN I TALKED ABOUT THAT TOO MUCH.
YOUR COFFEE.
HA HA - OF COURSE.
THANK YOU.

THEN, SHE WOULD BRING UP HOW I DIDN'T MAKE ANY MONEY, I SHOULD GO BACK TO SCHOOL, GET A BETTER JOB... BLAH BLAH BLAH BLAH...
BUT SHE KNEW YOU HAD A SHIT JOB WHEN YOU STARTED DATING.
I KNOW.

SO... BASICALLY, SHE DIDN'T WANT TO DATE A LOSER? RIGHT?
WELL, SHE DIDN'T SAY THAT!
COME ON, TRAVIS.

I KNOW, I KNOW. I'M DOING MY BEST NOT TO THINK ABOUT THAT PART OF IT.
IT'S PRETTY TERRIBLE.
UGH
I SAW HER YESTERDAY WHEN I WAS CLOSING UP THE SHOP.
THAT MUST HAVE SUCKED. HOW LONG HAS IT BEEN SINCE YOU'VE SEEN HER?
A COUPLE WEEKS, ACTUALLY. I THINK SHE WAS WITH SOMEONE.
WHOO BOY.
I THINK I'M AN ALCOHOLIC.
TRAVIS... WHAT THE FUCK? I HAVEN'T SEEN YOU IN MONTHS AND YOU LAY THIS ON ME?

LOOK... I-SORRY, I'M JUST KIND OF A MESS RIGHT NOW.
IT'S OKAY, TRAVIS. JUST FUCKIN' TAKE IT EASY. YOU'RE 37, MAN. I'M WORRIED ABOUT YOU.

I GOT THIS. WALK WITH ME, I HAVE TO GET TO WORK. I NEED TO POUND SOME THINGS INTO YOUR HUGE, THICK CRANIUM.

I FEEL TERRIBLE.
NOT AS TERRIBLE AS YOU'RE GOING TO!
DO TELL.

WE'RE GOING TO FIX STUART'S LAWN ON SATURDAY MORNING.

YOU HAVE TO BE KIDDING?
YOU'RE LUCKY THAT'S ALL YOU HAVE TO DO. I TALKED HIM DOWN FROM CALLING THE COPS, YOU DUMB SHIT.

FUCK MY LIFE.
LOOK, YOU DON'T HAVE A CHOICE. I MEAN, UNLESS YOU WANT TO BE CHARGED WITH DESTRUCTION OF PRIVATE PROPERTY.

YOU'RE RIGHT, YOU'RE RIGHT.
IT'S ONLY A FEW HOURS OF WORK TO MAKE UP FOR THE FACT THAT YOU ARE STUPID.

SO, JUST SUCK IT UP. YOU'RE PICKING ME UP AT 9 AM, BRIGHT AND EARLY!

YOU KNOW HOW I LIKE MY COFFEE.
YEAH, BLACK LIKE YOUR HEART.

SATURDAY...

Soooo....

WHAT'S ON YOUR MIND, RANDALL???
YOU SPOKEN TO MIKE LATELY?
SIGH

IT'S BEEN A LITTLE MORE THAN A YEAR. WHY DO YOU ASK?
JUST CURIOUS ABOUT HOW LONG YOU TWO ARE GOING TO HOLD A GRUDGE.
YOU WERE THERE THE LAST TIME WE SPOKE, MAN. NOT A GOOD SCENE.
I REMEMBER, BUT YOU GUYS HAVE BEEN FRIENDS FOR THE BETTER PART OF FIFTEEN YEARS.
THAT DOESN'T MATTER ANYMORE. I'VE GOTTEN MYSELF STUCK IN A RUT. THAT RUT IS DEEP, AND I'M STUCK! MY PLOW IS STUCK ON A BIG ROOT, AND I CAN'T MOVE!
THAT MAY BE THE DUMBEST THING I'VE EVER HEARD YOU SAY... EVER.
LIES
NO, REALLY!!

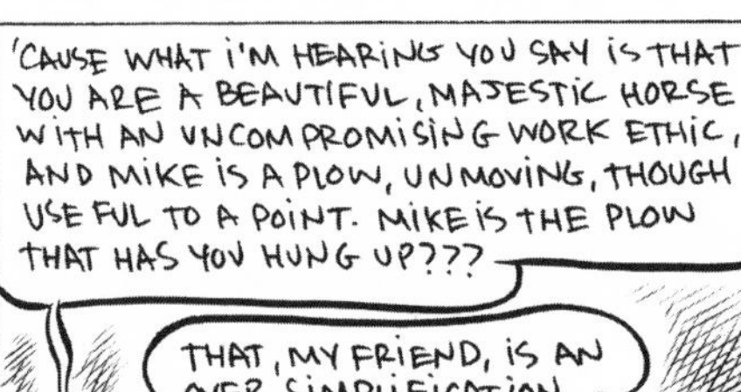
'CAUSE WHAT I'M HEARING YOU SAY IS THAT YOU ARE A BEAUTIFUL, MAJESTIC HORSE WITH AN UNCOMPROMISING WORK ETHIC, AND MIKE IS A PLOW, UNMOVING, THOUGH USEFUL TO A POINT. MIKE IS THE PLOW THAT HAS YOU HUNG UP???

THAT, MY FRIEND, IS AN OVER SIMPLIFICATION.

AT LEAST TELL ME YOU'RE NOT BLAMING HIM FOR ALL OF YOUR WOES, TRAVIS?
I'M NOT SAYING THAT, MAN.
I'VE LOST THE TRAIL THEN.

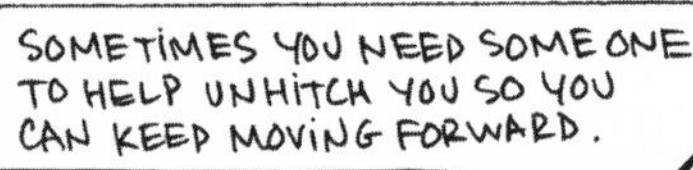

SOMETIMES YOU NEED SOMEONE TO HELP UNHITCH YOU SO YOU CAN KEEP MOVING FORWARD.
OH MY GOD... QUIT BEING SO FUCKING CONVOLUTED, MAN!

WHAT I'M SAYING IS THAT MIKE HAD ME STUCK, TO A POINT, BUT BECAUSE OF HIS INSUFFERABLE ATTITUDE, AND LUDICROUS BEHAVIOUR, HELPED ME GET UNHITCHED SO I COULD MOVE AHEAD.
YOU WANNA TALK ABOUT LUDICROUS? THAT LOGIC IS LUDICROUS.

YOU'RE FUCKED. LET'S CHANGE THE SUBJECT.
IT MAKES SENSE, FO SHIZZLE.
JUST KEEP YOUR EYES ON THE ROAD.
HOW ABOUT STUART??? THAT A GOOD SUBJECT?
HAHAHA YOU DON'T THINK I LIKED EVERYTHING MORE WHEN WE WERE JUST A BUNCH OF IDIOTS PLAYING MUSIC TOGETHER?
I THINK I'M GOING TO WRITE A BOOK ABOUT CHARLEY BUTTERS.
YOU'RE ACTUALLY CRAZY.

WHERE THE FUCK ARE THOSE TWO TROGLODYTES? MAKE ME WAIT ALL DAY?...ASSHOLES.
SON OF A BITCHES.
IT'S ABOUT TIME!
SHUT UP, YOU GARBAGE FACED DICK HEAD!
SHUT UP!!!
I'M NOT PLAYING DAD!!! BOTH OF YOU SHUT UP!!!

YOU! GO INSIDE, AND WE'LL FIX TRAVIS' MESS, OK?
GRMBL

YOU! GET THE TOOLS OUT OF THE TRUNK! NOW!
HRM

I'M DOING YOU A HUGE FAVOUR HERE. DON'T BE AN ASSHOLE, OK?
YOU'RE RIGHT! I'M SORRY.
DON'T LET HIM GET TO YOU.

BRRIIINGGG
BRRIIINGGG

WHAT THE FUCK?
WORK.
BRRiiiNGGG

DID YOU TALK TO MIKE?
WHAT? WHY?
BRRiiiNGGG

HE'S FUCKIN' CALLING RIGHT NOW!! YOU SAID SOMETHING TO HIM, DIDN'T YOU?!
NOPE.

UH... MIKE?

WAIT... WHAT?

...OH MY GOD...

YEAH, I'M ON MY WAY!

WHAT THE HELL, TRAVIS?!

AND SO...

MIKE?
MIKE?
MIKE...?
HM?

WHERE IS SHE?
...BEDROOM.

WHOOO...
OH BOY...

I'M GONNA CALL AN AMBULANCE. GO PACK SOME STUFF, YOU'LL STAY WITH ME FOR A LITTLE BIT.
YEAH.
UH... HELLO...

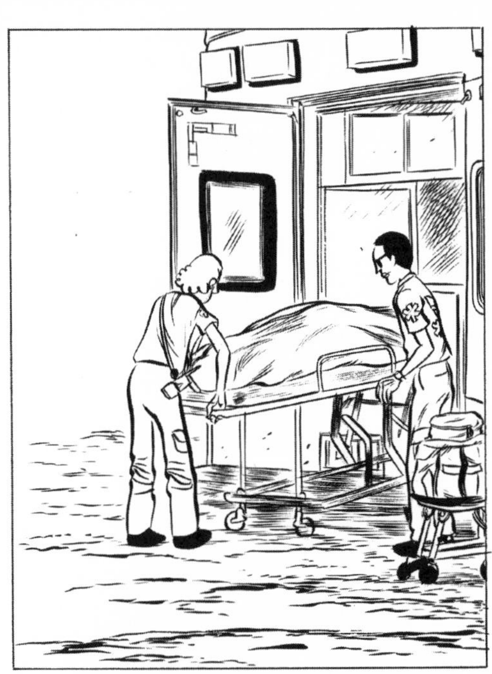

844

YOU OKAY, PAL?
I DON'T KNOW. I MEAN, THE LAST THING I THOUGHT I'D COME HOME TO WAS MY MOTHER - WELL, YOU KNOW...

SORRY MAN...
YEAH
HOW ABOUT WE GET OUTTA HERE?

THANKS, TRAVIS...
SHUT UP...

part three
"the death"

OCTOBER ...
GLK GLK GLK

...SIGH...

KIDS, SORRY I'M LATE. LINE UP AT THE COFFEE SHOP.
HEY TRAVIS. NO WORRIES.
HEY PAL.
JESUS, DAVE... WHAT THE--
JUST CHECKING THAT YOU AREN'T BOOZING AGAIN. WHAT'S THAT SMELL?
SNF SNF SNF
C'MON DAVE, IT'S JUST THE MOUTH WASH I'M USING NOW.
...OK... WE HAD A DEAL, TRAVIS.
I KNOW, I HAVEN'T FORGOTTEN. I'M GONNA HANG UP MY JACKET.
IS HE STILL DRINKING?
I THINK SO, BUT CAN'T BE SURE.
GODDAMN ALCOHOLICS.

EVERYTHING'S FINE...

LATER...
YOU COOL IF I HEAD OUT? MY BOY FRIEND IS JUST OUTSIDE.
YEAH, I CAN HANDLE THE NO CUSTOMERS TODAY.
ALRIGHT, MAN. SMELL YA LATER.
HA HA YEAH, SAY HI TO PATRICK FOR ME.
X-RAY RECORDS

DON'T MIND IF I DO!
FUCK.
LATER...

SCRAPEE:

CHK
KA-CHK

HEY BUDDY! JUST GETTIN' IN, 'EH?! HOUND DOG OF LOVE OVER HERE!!

WHAT THE FUCK HAPPENED TO YOU??? WHAT HAPPENED TO YOUR FUCKIN' TOOTH???
AHHH, IT'S NOTHING!
WHAT DO YOU MEAN BY "NOTHING"?

WHATEVER, MAN. I MAY HAVE FALLEN OVER LAST NIGHT.
THE BITTER IRONING, EH TRAVIS!

IRONY, YOU MEAN, AND THIS IS NOT THE LEAST BIT IRONIC... AT ALL!
YEAH! A YEAR AGO, I WAS THE IRRESPONSIBLE ONE. NOW IT'S YOU!
THAT'S NOT EVEN A LITTLE BIT IRONIC.
ISN'T IT?

LOOK, WHATEVER, HELP ME GET MY SHIT OUTSIDE.
OH YEAH... YOU READY TO GO HOME? THERE'S NO RUSH, MAN. YOU KNOW THAT.

IT'S BEEN LIKE THREE MONTHS. I REALLY WANT TO SLEEP IN MY BED.
FAIR ENOUGH.

MY DOOR'S ALWAYS OPEN, MICHAEL.
THANKS, TRAV. I APPRECIATE EVERYTHING.
AND LAY OFF THE SAUCE A LITTLE, WOULDJA? YOU'RE STARTING TO REALLY WORRY ME.
RIGHT.

I HEAR GREEN TEA WILL REALLY FUCK YOU UP.

RIGHT... GREEN TEA...

FUCK ME.

3B

FSSHT

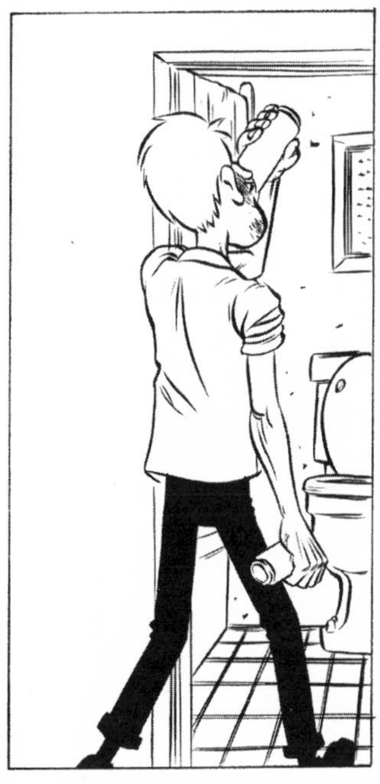

HOW DO I EXPLAIN THIS?

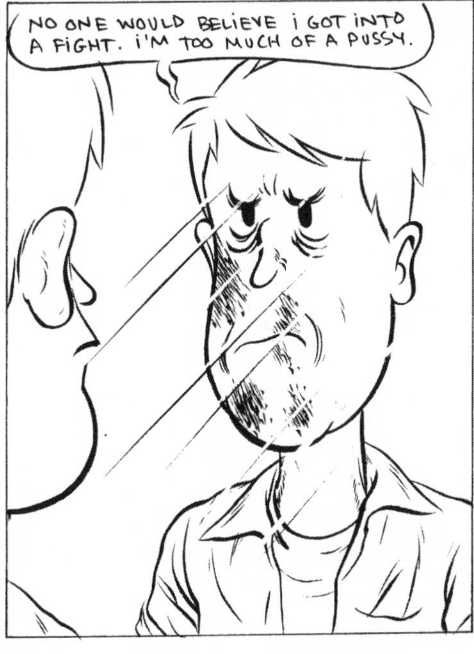
NO ONE WOULD BELIEVE I GOT INTO A FIGHT. I'M TOO MUCH OF A PUSSY.

HOPE NO ONE NOTICES.
AND SO...
MORNIN' TRAVIS.
UH, MORNIN' DAVE!
HOW'S IT GOIN' TODAY, TRAVIS?
FEELIN' FINE.

WHAT DID YOU GET UP TO LAST NIGHT? I WENT TO SEE BLOODSHOT BILL... HAD A FEW TOO MANY! WHOO BOY!
OH DAMN. I FORGOT HE WAS PLAYING!

OH Y'KNOW... JUST HAD A QUIET, UNEVENTFUL NIGHT IN. WATCHED SOME ROCKFORD FILES RERUNS, AND THAT'S ABOUT IT.
OH MAN! I LOVE THE ROCKFORD FILES. WHICH EPISODE?

UHHH -- THE ONE WHERE ROCKFORD LOSES THE GIRL AND GETS--
LOOK AT ME, TRAVIS.
--SCREWED OVER.

MM-HMM?
GODDAMMIT, TRAVIS.

FUCK.

WHAT HAPPENED? AND DON'T LIE TO ME ANY MORE.

I DON'T KNOW. I WOKE UP FACE DOWN ON THE SIDEWALK.
JESUS CHRIST, TRAVIS. YOU KNOW I HAVE TO FIRE YOU, RIGHT?
C'MON, DAVE!

WE HAD A DEAL! YOU PAID ME BACK, AND I'M GRATEFUL FOR THAT, BUT YOU HAD TO QUIT DRINKING! YOU REEK OF BEER, AND IT'S ONLY ELEVEN IN THE MORNING!
GIMME ANOTHER SHOT! I PROMISE I'LL STOP DRINKING THIS TIME!

JUST GET OUT.

LATER...
UH...CHEF, THERE'S A DRUNK GUY AT THE BAR WHO SAYS HE KNOWS YOU.
WHO IS IT?
SOME BLONDE GUY MISSING A FRONT TOOTH ...I DON'T KNOW.
THANKS.

...MISSING TOOTH?

JUST GIMME A FUCKIN' DRINK, Y'FUCKIN' POTATO HEAD!

GET THIS GUY OUTTA HERE!

IT'S OK, I'VE GOT MY OWN!!!

C'MON TRAVIS!

YOU KNOW THIS GUY?!

I'M TAKING CARE OF IT!

WHAT IS GOING ON WITH YOU, TRAVIS?
HWWC RGHK

BWOOOOOORRRFFF

I HATE MYSELF, RANDALL.
I KNOW, BUDDY.

JESUS FUCKING CHRIST...

Lumberking
Home Improvement Centre

HEY BUDDY, WHAT'S SO URGENT?
I'M GOING AWAY FOR A LITTLE WHILE.
WHAT THE HELL'S GOING ON, TRAVIS?
WHERE'S YOUR JACKET?
IT'S IN-UH-THE CAR. YOU AND RANDALL MAN, JEEZ.

I'M A FUCKIN' MESS, MIKE. I HAVE TO LEAVE.
JESUS CHRIST, WHAT HAPPENED?
GOT FIRED... EVERYTHING IS HORRIBLE.

I-UH... HMM... WHERE ARE YOU GOING?
TRAVIS?

HEH HEH

TRAVIS...?

YOU'RE GOING TO THAT CABIN, AREN'T YOU?
IT'S ALL I'VE GOT, MAN!!!

I'LL COME BACK IN A FEW WEEKS. HERE'S MY KEYS.
IT'S NOT A GOOD IDEA FOR YOU TO GO THERE, TRAVIS.

I'LL BE FINE, THANKS, MIKE.
I DON'T LIKE THIS.

LOOK, DON'T WORRY ABOUT IT. I'LL HAVE EVERYTHING I NEED. THERE'S A GENERAL STORE CLOSE BY... NO BOOZE, SO... THERE YOU GO.
ALRIGHT. CALL ME AND RANDALL SO WE KNOW YOU'RE OK.

YOU'VE GOT IT, PAL!
I DON'T LIKE IT!

AFTERNOON.
HEY.
MAPS
KEYS CUT
Old Dutch

15
FLOUR
FLOUR
FLOUR

YOU LOOK FAMILIAR...

I WAS HERE BACK IN THE SUMMER, LOOKING FOR THAT PAINTER.

SHIT! THAT WAS YOU?

HAHA YEAH.

WELL, PARDON MY CANDOR, BUT YOU LOOK WORSE FOR WEAR! YOU MISSING A TOOTH THERE? WHAT HAPPENED TO YOU?

CAN I USE THAT ONE?! IT'S A GOOD LINE!
WASN'T REALLY A JOKE, BUT HAVE AT 'ER.
C'MON, THAT HAD TO HAVE BEEN A JOKE!
NOPE.
OH BOO HOO HOOO LIFE'S SO HARD ON ME!
HRMF!
WHAT THE FUCK, LADY???
I CAN TELL BY LOOKING AT YOU THAT YOU'VE HAD SOME BAD LUCK, BUT DON'T COME IN HERE TALKING ABOUT HARDSHIP. I WON'T HEAR IT.
I'VE LOST MY PATIENCE WITH YOU, KID. YOU WANT ANY THING ELSE?
LOOK, I'M SURE YOU'VE SUFFERED WORSE THAN I HAVE, BUT I'VE HAD A PRETTY ROUGH YEAR! NOW MAYBE I'M BEING A TAD OVERLY DRAMATIC, BUT SHIT...
A MAN CAN ONLY TAKE SO MUCH! I LOST MY GODDAMN TOOTH!!!
MAN ALIVE.

CAN I GET YOU SOMETHING ELSE?
≡SIGH≡ YOU CARRY BOOZE YET?
NO! GROCERY STORE.
JESUS CHRIST... GIMME A CARTON OF CIGARETTES.

NOW FUCK OFF.

I USED TO THINK YOU WERE COOL. IT'S NOT A COMPETITION TO SEE WHO'S HAD IT WORSE, Y'BATTLE AXE!

AND SO...
YEAH, AND I GOT MY BOOZE, NO THANKS TO YOU, YOU OLD BAT!!!

≡MMBL≡ OLD BAG GRMBL

I'M DONE!!!

I'M FUCKING DONE!!!

FUCK FUCK FUCK

HUFF HUFF HUFF

AW SHIT... I FORGOT ABOUT ALL THIS...

BEER

I CAN DO THIS!!!

~HRM~

FUCK FUCK FUCK

HRM

GODDAMMIT

FUCK it

AND SO...
I DON'T EVEN KNOW WHAT YOU'RE GOING ON ABOUT ANYMORE... YOU'RE JUST A FUCKIN' ASSHOLE, AREN'T YOU, CHARLEY?
WHAT DOES IT EVEN MATTER? CHUG
...FUGGIN'... STUPID...
CHUG

... SO FUGGIN' HOT!!!

HOLY SHIT!!!

SoB SoB SoB SoB

WHAT THE FUCK DID YOU DO, KID?

I KNEW THE GUY WHO HAD THAT CABIN. YOU BURNED IT DOWN!

... YOU KNEW HIM?

YOU KNEW CHARLEY BUTTERS?
A LITTLE BIT.

FUCK... FUCK... YOU KNEW CHARLEY.
WHAT'S WRONG WITH YOU?
I'M AN ALCOHOLIC, I RUIN EVERY-THING...

EVERYTHING.
OK

WELL... NO USE CRYIN' OVER SPILLED MILK... UM, WHAT WAS YOUR NAME?
...TRAVIS.
RIGHT. BILL.
YOU'RE BILL...?
JUST SAID THAT.
YOU COMING?
OR YOU CAN GO BACK TO WHEREVER YOU CAME FROM.
WHERE ARE WE GOING?
EAT SOME STEW. SOBER YOU UP.
YEAH.

GO HAVE A SEAT. I'LL MAKE US SOME COFFEE.

ISN'T IT A LITTLE LATE FOR COFFEE?
5 AM. SUN'LL BE UP SOON, KID.

DO YOU DRINK COFFEE?
WELL, YEAH, BUT--
WOULD YOU DRINK SOME COFFEE?
YES.
THANK YOU.

CHNK
KLATTER
So, HOW'D YOU KNOW CHARLEY?
WE WERE NEIGHBOURS, I GUESS YOU COULD SAY. THAT'S OBVIOUS, THOUGH.

WHAT DO YOU MEAN?
YOU KNOW EXACTLY WHAT I MEAN. LOOK, I MAY BE OUT HERE ON MY OWN, NO ONE TO TALK TO, BUT I CAN CERTAINLY TELL WHEN SOMEONE IS DANCING AROUND A SUBJECT.

BEEN ALONE A LONG TIME, BUT I THINK IT'S MADE ME MORE KEENLY AWARE OF ORDINARY PEOPLE'S BULLSHIT... ORDINARY FUCKIN' PEOPLE.
I'M NOT TRYING TO BULLSHIT, BUT I GUESS I WAS DANCIN' AROUND...

IS HE DEAD?
OH GOD YES!

WH-WH-WHAT? WHEN?
GOTTA BE '65.
...1965???

WHY ARE YOU OUT HERE?
TRYING TO FIGURE OUT WHAT HAPPENED TO CHARLEY.
BUT WHY? ARE YOU A PRIVATE INVESTIGATOR?
WELL, NO...
WELL, WHAT THEN?

I WAS MAKING A DOCUMENTARY ABOUT HIM, BUT IT ALL FELL APART.
WHAT THE HELL IS A DOCUMENTARY?
OH... RIGHT.
PRKLE PRKL PRKL

IT'S LIKE A NON-FICTION MOVIE.
HUH... GOOD IDEA.
SOMETIMES.

WHAT WAS SO INTERESTING ABOUT OL' CHARLEY?
HERE, DRINK THIS COFFEE.
HE WAS ABOUT TO BECOME A FAMOUS PAINTER, AND HE JUST LEFT IT ALL BEHIND. NO ONE KNEW WHAT HAPPENED TO HIM.

WELL SHIT. NOTHING TO TELL, KID.

HE'S JUST DEAD.

THERE HAS TO BE MORE TO IT THAN THAT!!!
BULLSHIT!
WHY BULLSHIT?!
BECAUSE HE DIDN'T HAVE A CLUE ABOUT HOW TO SURVIVE!

MAYBE HE WAS CRAZY, i DON'T KNOW. i DIDN'T TAKE THE TIME TO GET TO KNOW THAT! WHAT i DO KNOW IS THAT HE WAS FUCKIN' CLUE-LESS, KID, KINDA LIKE YOU.
i'M CLUELESS?!
YOU'RE DAMN RIGHT!

FOLLOW ME.
YOU ARE AN ASSHOLE, OLD MAN.
NOPE. i JUST DON'T SUFFER FOOLS. NOW C'MON, IT'S JUST OVER HERE.

WHAT THE HELL iS THIS?

THIS iS CHARLEY.

...UM-WHAT'S THAT?
I BURIED CHARLEY RIGHT HERE.
WHAT THE FUCK ARE YOU TALKING ABOUT, MAN?
ARE YOU STUPID?

GOD, NO WONDER YOU'RE OUT HERE ALL ALONE. NOW JUST TELL ME THE FUCKIN' STORY!!!
ALRIGHT, SHUT UP!

IT'S NOT A VERY INTERESTING STORY... NOT MANY OF THEM ARE, IN REALITY...

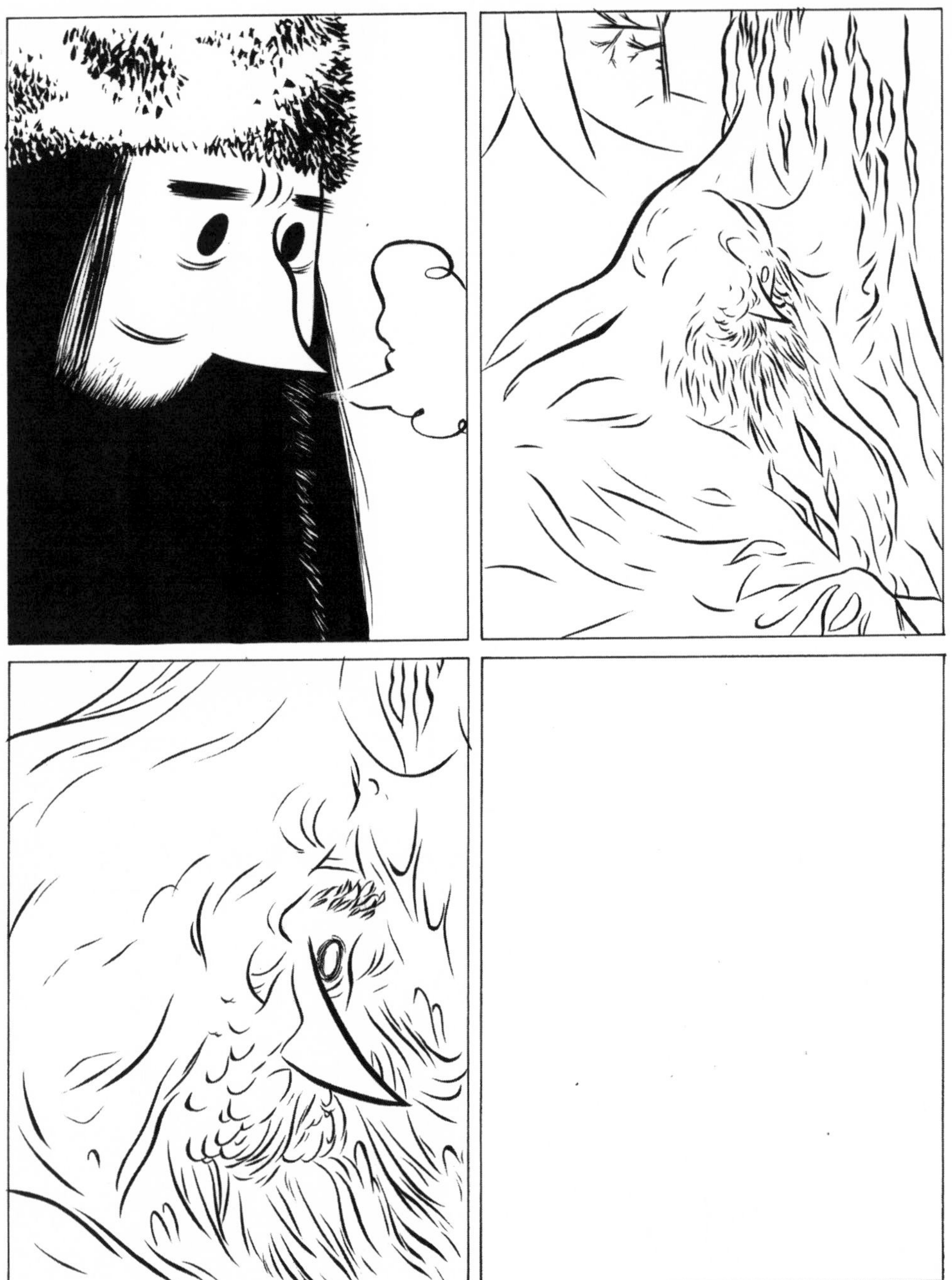

...THE FUCK?!
THAT'S WHAT I FUCKED EVERYTHING UP FOR?
'FRAID SO.

...THAT'S IT...?

THAT'S IT???
YEP.

CAN i GET A HIT OFF THAT FLASK?
GLK GLK GLK

I'VE GOTTA GO.

WELL, FUCK YOU.

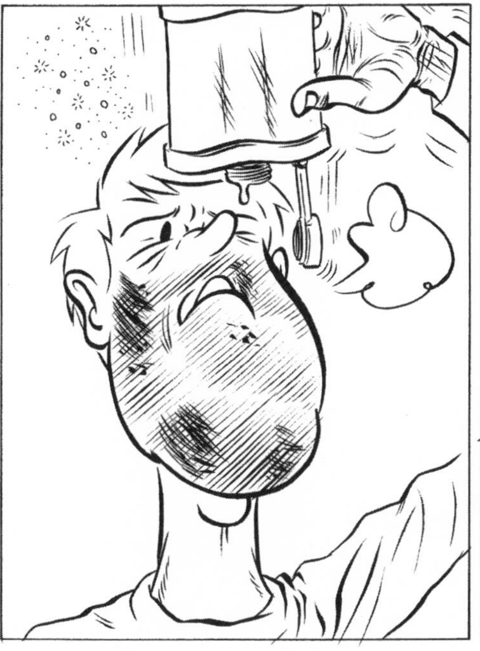

FUCK.

FUCK! FUCK! FUCK! THERE'S GOTTA BE A BOTTLE IN HERE!

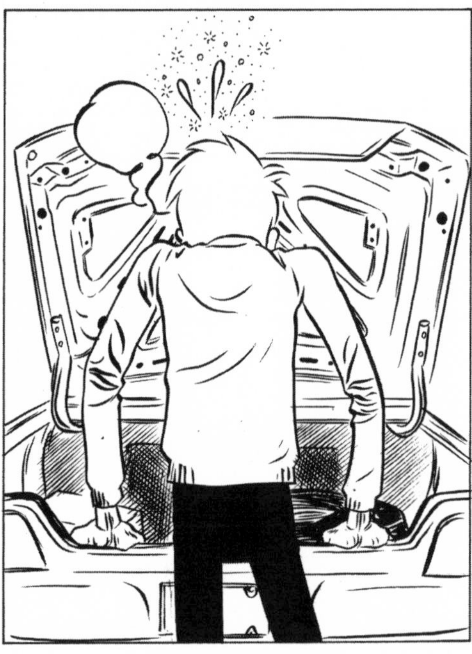

GENERAL No 12

CREEAAKKKK

KLNK
KNK

CLNK
SHUFF

JUST HOLD ON THERE!!!
WAAHH!!!

DNK

OH MY GOD!!!
DID I KILL HIM???

SHIT!!!

LITTLE SHIT!!!

HOLY FUCK!!!
PAW
PAW

JESUS CHRIST!!!

FWEEEENN
SSSHHHHTTT
TSSHHH
PAW

GOT HIS LICENSE PLATE, GODDAMMIT!!!
WALKING STICKS
ALL NATURAL
HANDCUT
$20

ABOUT FIFTEEN MILES AWAY...
SCREEECHHH

MOTHERFUCKER!!!
HOLY FUCKIN' SHIT!!!
JESUS FUCK!!!

WHAT THE SHITTING FUCK AM I GOING TO DO?

THIS IS IT.
...THE FUCK?!

KNK KNK KNK

WHF

C'MON PAL! OUTTA THE CAR!!!

SQUEAK
SQUEAK
SQUEAK

SIR, COULD YOU--
SQUEAK

OH MY GOD!!!
DISGUSTING.

SIR, STEP OUT OF THE CAR!
UH, OH, OK... YEAH SURE.

SIR! HANDS OFF THE WHEEL, AND STEP OUT OF THE CAR SLOWLY!!
NOW!!
HEH HEH

OUT OF THE CAR!!! NOW!!!

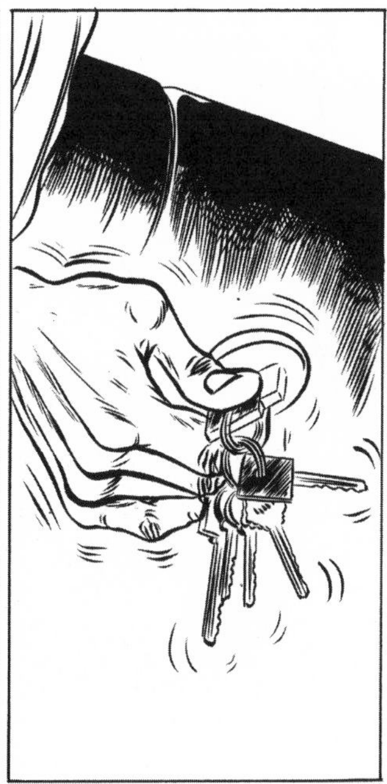

HURRY THE HECK UP!!!
GODDAMMIT!

WHAT-THE-FUCK???

FUCK!!!

BEEYOO BEEYOO
JESUS CHRIST!!!

I'M FUCKED... I'M SO FUCKED!!!

GODDAMMIT!!!
PUNCH
PUNCH
PUNCH
PUNCH

CHUG
GUG
CHGG

FUCK YOU, YOU FUCKIN' PIGS!!! YOU'LL NEVER FUCKIN' TAKE ME ALIVE!!!

GLG
GLG
GLG

CRUNCH
WEE-OOO-WEE
OOO-WHEE-OOO

FUUUUUUUUCKK

WHAT?

WHEN WAS THE LAST TIME YOU SAW TRAVIS? I MEAN, I SAW HIM LIKE THREE WEEKS AGO, HE WAS ROUGH, BUT...

HE WAS BEYOND ROUGH WHEN I LAST SAW HIM. I SHOULD'VE SEEN THIS COMING... I REALLY SHOULD HAVE.
HOW COULD YOU HAVE?

I MEAN, JESUS CHRIST!

SIGH ... WELL, WE'RE HERE.
THIS IS SO FUCKED UP.

WHAT CAN I DO YA FOR, HUH?

WHAT'S THE STATE OF YOUR BUSINESS?
VISITING A PRISONER.
NAME OF INMATE?
TRAVIS LEE LEWIS.

REALLY? THAT'S HIS NAME?
ROCKABILLY PARENTS.
...ALRIGHT. LET ME SEE YOUR I.D., SON.
WHAT KIND OF NAME IS HYVÄRINEN?
IT'S FINNISH.

HUH! I DON'T KNOW ANYTHING ABOUT FINNISH PEOPLE.
...REALLY...?
YOU BLUBBER EATERS?
JESUS! CAN WE GO IN NOW, PLEASE?
MR. SENSITIVE! WHO YOU GOT THERE WITH YOU? MICHAEL HERMAN?!
YEAH, BUT DON'T MAKE FUN OF MY NAME, 'CAUSE MY MOM JUST DIED.
I-UH... OK, GO ON THROUGH.
...AND ENJOY YOUR VISIT.

AND SO...

BBZZZZTTT

HOW THE HELL ARE YOU DOING, TRAVIS?

ARE YOU IN A GANG YET???

I'M-UH-OK, GUYS. I MEAN, THIS WAS THE BEST OUTCOME FOR ALL THE SHIT I CAUSED, RIGHT?

I THINK QUITTING DRINKING WOULD HAVE BEEN THE BEST OUTCOME!!!

YEAH, RANDALL IS RIGHT.

i ROBBED A STORE, ATTACKED AN OLD MAN, HIT A COP WITH MY CAR, GOT SHOT AT... i DRUNKENLY DROVE MY CAR INTO A DITCH... THEY EVEN THREW VAGRANCY ONTO THE LIST OF CHARGES... AND THAT'S JUST THE LAST MONTH! FORGET EVERY-THING ELSE THAT'S HAPPENED.

i TOTALLY DESERVE THIS. AT LEAST i CAN POTENTIALLY GET A REDUCED SENTENCE IF i GET COUNCELLING, AND GO TO PRISON REHAB. i MEAN SHIT.... REHAB IN PRISON...
DAMN... i CAN'T EVEN WRAP MY HEAD AROUND ALL OF THIS.
YEAH...

i NEED A FUCKIN' DRINK. i REALLY NEED A DRINK. i'M LOSING IT IN HERE.
62131125152

PSST! HEY!
62131125

I'VE GOT A FAVOUR TO ASK YOU GUYS.

YEAH, WHAT IS IT, TRAVIS?

IT'S REALLY, REALLY IMPORTANT!
ANYTHING, BUDDY!

YOU GUYS HAVE TO BREAK ME OUTTA HERE!!!...

I NEED A DRINK.

6213112251521
6213112251521

621311251521